INC. MY DREAM

A God Inspired Process to Turn Your BIG
Idea Into a Dream Business

PAUL WILSON, JR.

Kingdom Business University
Atlanta, Georgia

Inc. My Dream: A God Inspired Process to Turn Your BIG Idea Into a Dream Business
by Paul Wilson, Jr.

Printed in the United States of America

Printed by CreateSpace, An Amazon.com Company

Available from Amazon.com and other online stores.

ISBN-10: 0692263217
ISBN-13: 978-0692263211

www.KingdomBusinessUniversity.com

DEDICATION

I am truly blessed with an amazing, loving family. This book is dedicated to Shawnice, my incredible wife whose unyielding support would not let me give up on my dreams. This book is also dedicated to my awesome children, Soraya, Paul III, Sophia, and Perez, part of the next generation of B.I.G. dreamers and doers who will change the world!

PAUL WILSON, JR.

"For a dream comes through the multitude of business…"
Ecclesiastes 5:3 (KJV)

"Hope deferred makes the heart sick, but a dream fulfilled is a tree of life."
Proverbs 13:12 (NLT)

"… Engage in business until I come."
Luke 19:13

INC. MY DREAM

CONTENTS

INC. MY DREAM

FOREWORD

The Breath of God

Even as you read these words, breath is entering and leaving your body. But most people rarely pay attention to breathing until or unless it is elevated by exercise or triggered by a lung disorder. In like manner, scores of otherwise gifted and talented people live their lives rarely ever noticing the breath of God within them. Routinely ignoring the still small voice of God, people who are destined for more, tend to run out of breath for their dreams, opting to settle for doing little with the much they have been given.

Thank God for Paul Wilson's *Inc My Dream*. This book will pump life into your vision, revive your enthusiasm and restore the confidence you need to wake up in your dreams. Unlike the books on entrepreneurialism, which highlight me, myself and I, you will be challenged to do more than make money. The reader will gain a sense of community responsibility, receive a charge to help others, and will be urged to emulate the strength of the Mind of Christ.

Christians who are stuck in the foyer of church politics, titles and labels, will find an exit ramp to escape religion after reading each chapter. Entrepreneurs who are looking to grow both personally and professionally, will find it refreshing to re-embrace their call to the marketplace. Those who need next steps will receive clarity and folks who want to develop the next generation will find a platform upon which to build.

You just might get your life back, your groove back, after reading *Inc My Dream*. At the very least you will be made to pay attention to where you are in your current journey and inspired to step up your game. This compilation will raise your heart rate for your life's work and increase the way you process your end product for God's planet. It's now time to be coached into your next level; the world needs to know what you think by the actions you live and *Inc*.

J. Calvin Tibbs

INC. MY DREAM

INTRODUCTION

Kingdom Calling

"Unless the Lord builds the house, the builders labor in vain…"
Psalm 127:1

The Greatest Commission

As his time was expiring on the planet, Jesus gives a final charge to his disciples before he returns to Heaven in what most Christians refer to as the "Great Commission":

> *"Then Jesus came to them and said, 'All authority in heaven and on earth has been given to me. Therefore go and make disciples of all nations, baptizing them in the name of the Father and of the Son and of the Holy Spirit, and teaching them to obey everything I have commanded you. And surely I am with you always, to the very end of the age.'"* Matthew 28:18-20

This command was not only a commission for the disciples and us, it was also a "co-mission" because Jesus promised that he would always be present to lead, teach, comfort, and empower us through the Holy Spirit, so that we can successfully complete our assigned mission of advancing God's Kingdom.

Kingdom building entrepreneurs are purpose driven business leaders who accept the responsibility and opportunity to integrate the Great Commission into the planning, development, and execution of their business operations. The dream business idea God placed in your heart is connected to your purpose, which is also connected to fixing or reconciling a problem in the earth that He wants solved. Kingdom entrepreneurs are "about our Father's business" of transforming lives. This is not a career. It is a calling. This type of venture closely resembles the growing global missions outreach movement called Business as Mission / Ministry (BAM).

You must embrace the fact that you were designed and shaped for a specific purpose for a specific time to reach a specific people. This is your time!

Inc. My Dream Objectives

Key objectives that will be accomplished in this book include:

⇨ Recognize how to align your life mission/calling with your business aspirations.

⇨ Understand the key components and strategic processes for establishing and operating a co-mission driven business with excellence.

⇨ Identify marketplace opportunities in which to effectively deploy your gifts and talents.

⇨ Understand the strategic role and opportunity for co-mission driven businesses to impact our communities.

V-STAR Business Planning System

Every well-run organization has an operations manual by which they establish the rules and regulations that everyone must follow in order to produce success. Furthermore every organization has a culture, made up of formal and informal customs, behaviors, beliefs, norms, and other characteristics that set the tone or the atmosphere that they believe to be the most conducive for all those who work there.

The Pentateuch, or the Books of the Law, was the set of rules and regulations that God established for the Hebrews to govern and manage how they were to interact with Himself and one another. The Law also helped to establish their culture, i.e. religious customs and social norms that would stay with the Jewish people throughout history even until today. Furthermore, God set these in place for His people to understand what would draw His blessings for obedience and the punishment for disobedience.

One of the key themes of these books is holiness, which means to be "set apart" or "sacred." Today many Christians have an incorrect belief that church activities are sacred but business is secular. They often think preaching, singing, and other similar gifts used in church are more anointed than Christians who operate in business in the marketplace everyday. *"The earth is the Lord's and the fullness thereof, and they that dwell within"* (Psalm 24:1), which means that even business is sacred when it is done as unto the Lord (Colossians 3:23-24). God's wants to get the glory out of everything that He calls us to. You and your business are called to be set apart and sacred to the Lord.

This book introduces the V-STAR Business Planning System, a God inspired process which will help you transform your God-idea into a profitable entrepreneurial venture that is built on Biblical principles and utilizes today's business best practices. This is a comprehensive planning tool that should not only be used for your initial planning, but should also be used as an on-going strategic planning platform.

Vision, Mission, & Values
What & Why?

Results — Measures?

C.O.R.E. Focus

Strategy — How?

Action Planning — What & When?

Target Market — Who?

Did you know that your spiritual gifts were not just to be used at church? In Ephesians 4:11-12 Apostle Paul explains, *"And he gave the apostles, the prophets, the evangelists, the shepherds[c] and teachers, to equip the saints for the work of ministry, for building up the body of Christ."* If you notice, there is nothing here or any other place in Scripture to indicate that your spiritual gifts were only to be used at church. In fact, each of these five-fold ministry gifts has a marketplace correlation for their spiritual function. One key distinctions of the V-STAR Business Planning System is the fact that the functions of the five-fold ministry are embedded in this model. Let's take a look:

V-STAR & Five-Fold Ministry Functions

V-STAR Function	Five-Fold Ministry	Marketplace Function
Vision, Mission, & Values	Apostle	The visionary entrepreneur business owner who establishes businesses throughout his customer demographic and directs the vision of his company.
Strategy	Prophet	The company consultant or upper management persons consulted for important matters of the business and who influences the business owner with researched understanding that helps guide appropriate company decision making.
Target Market	Evangelist	Marketing, advertising, public relations, customer service. Employees in the workplace should be operating as an evangelist of their company.
Action Planning	Pastor	Function as managers over departments and groups to make sure the leaders plans are carried out as instructed and successfully but always mindful of the needs of his people.
Results Management	Teacher	The role of one whose wisdom, experience and learning is utilized to assure productivity, efficiency resulting in ROI to the company.

While some of the roles are definitely interchangeable, there is a strong correlation between these five components and the specific ministry gifts identified by Paul. So as you can clearly see this goes much deeper than your typical business planning tool. And although I present lots of information and concepts in this book, this is still a streamlined way of viewing your Kingdom enterprise. In the Appendix I included a Quick Start Business Planning Questionnaire that summarizes a lot of the content contained throughout this book.

Kingdom Building Entrepreneur Characteristics

The Nazarite Vow, described in Numbers 6, was an opportunity for men and woman to separate unto God for specific service. They committed to certain hygiene, dietary, and cultural standards above and beyond what God was requiring of everyone else. Due to their devotion and discipline God's special anointing was on them.

Although God is not asking you to take a Nazarite Vow per se, He does expect you to separate from the world's ways of thinking and doing things. As a Kingdom marketplace priest God is expecting a life of devotion to Him. The benefit you receive is that purity positions you for His power. Those who walk holy before God are prepared and postured to be used greatly by Him in the marketplace and beyond.

God always establishes certain criteria when He appoints leaders to carry out His purposes. The same can be said for Kingdom building entrepreneurs. Characteristics of Kingdom building entrepreneurs include:

- ✓ Kingdom driven
- ✓ Resourceful and business oriented
- ✓ Passionate visionary
- ✓ Purpose driven
- ✓ Dynamic and influential
- ✓ Creative and practical
- ✓ Proactive and positive

When you accept the call to Kingdom leadership, God is expecting more from you in terms of abiding by His principles because you are influencing others. It may seem unfair, but *"to whom much is given, much is required."* God's rules are not meant to restrict you, but to protect and perfect you. The boundaries He establishes for your life and leadership will bring out the best in you through disciplined practice. Additionally, they are going to benefit you by keeping you focused on the things He deems most important. Leaders that are undisciplined or get distracted are leaders that usually fall into sin or out of the will of God. Embracing His rules allow you to experience His best for you.

Kingdom entrepreneurs are disciplined, submitted, heavenly focused change agents. So now that you know you have a choice…

"Lead, follow, or get out of the way!"

The Power to Get Wealth

God is The Creator and by divine dispensation we are creators also. God doesn't need money, but we need it to accomplish the work He's commissioned us to do in the earth. God doesn't leave it up to chance or circumstance for you to get what's required for you to accomplish your assignment. He gave you real power to create or take advantage of opportunities to acquire wealth. Unfortunately many people, including Christians, have a misperception of wealth and thereby repel it, or they attract it with the wrong intentions. These few points will bring some clarification:

1) God owns all the wealth in the world. When it's in our possession, it's only as a steward.
2) God gave you the ability to get wealth, so He must also desire that you have it (within some specific parameters).
3) God is the source of your wealth, not you, a job, business, or anything/anyone else.
4) Money should be seen as a tool that serves you, not a god that you worship.
5) Having lots of money will not keep you out of heaven. Only the lack of a real relationship with Jesus can do that.
6) God connected His purposes with your prosperity to establish His covenant in the earth. Your job is to use it to invest in the growth of God's family through churches, ministries, businesses, and other means.

God's blessings are measured by more than just dollars and cents. Money is the floor of our blessings, not the ceiling as many people mistakenly perceive it to be. God's greatest blessings are found in His presence, i.e. love, acceptance, peace, faith, joy, wisdom, revelation, purpose, power, courage, patience, grace, mercy, creativity, discernment, and more. When you are operating at a high level of abundance in these areas (receiving and giving), money will easily flow to you as a side benefit.

Opportunities for Impact

The Christian walk is intended to be very interactive. You cannot be an effective Christian while living on a relationship island. That is why God has placed each of within groups and environments that require us to engage with people. Your opportunities for direct or indirect impact can be divided into five interconnected circles of influence…

1) **Personal**: your individual self, including your mind, body, and spirit.
2) **Faith / Church**: your core values/belief system; place of worship.
3) **Family**: your immediate family and relatives.

4) **Career**: your profession where you apply your skills and derive income.
5) **Community**: whomever you have a natural affinity with or regular association (i.e. friends, geographic, ethnic, socioeconomic, or others).

Raising the Quality of Life for Others

The Gospel has the power to transform lives, but if we never take it outside of our church services and to the people in our communities who need it the most, they may never have the opportunity to experience God's power. Kingdom entrepreneurs are problem-solvers that use their businesses as platforms to bring positive changes to the places where God positions them to serve.

Dr. Martin Luther King, Jr. said it best as he described the practical role that the Gospel is to play to combat the challenges that are faced everyday in our cities and communities:

"The gospel at its best deals with the whole man, not only with his soul but also his body, not only his spiritual well-being but also his material well-being. A religion that professes a concern for the souls of men and is not equally concerned about the slums that damn them, the economic conditions that strangle them and the social conditions that cripple them is a dry-as-dust religion."

Kingdom entrepreneurs have the potential to decrease the potency of the kingdom of darkness in our neighborhoods, communities, and cities, which will result in a higher quality of life, naturally and spiritually. Specific areas where we should see direct results from our efforts include:

✓ Crime
✓ Homelessness
✓ Educational system
✓ Illiteracy
✓ Sex slavery / trafficking
✓ Physical and mental health
✓ Poor lifestyle choices
✓ Poverty
✓ Unemployment
✓ School dropouts
✓ Spiritual depravity
✓ Teen Pregnancy
✓ Unemployment
✓ Other areas

You have the opportunity as a Kingdom CEO to be a transformational agent in people's lives in one or more of these areas. Are you willing to take the challenge of not just being a financially successful entrepreneur, but to be a Kingdom leader who helps deliver people out of spiritual slavery?

* * * * *

"A Kingdom business disrupts the enemy's economy."
~Candace Ford

* * * * *

If God called you to be an entrepreneur, He ordained you to be a priest in the marketplace, interceding for the needs and issues of leaders, employees, customers, and many others. This allows you to hear from God so you can speak life into all those you come into contact with. Your ministry happens every day of the week, not just on Sundays. You are on the spiritual front lines with the grand opportunity to transfer wealth into the Kingdom and disrupt the enemy's plans.

Exponential Potential

When you consider the network of people that God has connected you with, the opportunity that you have to impact people's lives is exponential. Think of your customers, and their friends and families and their friends and families and on and on. Directly influencing one person to live a better life could lead to you indirectly affecting hundreds, thousands, or even millions. Think about the person that led Billie Graham to Christ. Most people don't even know his name, but his legacy is monumental!

In order to help you achieve your exponential potential, certain foundational principles will guide us through the rest of this book...

⇨ You are a CEO, "Christ's Executive Officer." You and your business belong to Him. He has anointed and appointed you to lead well as a "Creator of Economic Opportunity." This is so much bigger than just you owning your own business.

⇨ Don't take this calling to marketplace ministry lightly. Many are called but few are chosen to go into the marketplace to advance the Kingdom. It is just as important as pastoring or being a missionary. Your pulpit, i.e. mission field, just happens to be offices, cubicles, boardrooms, coffee shops, in the community, or online. You don't have a second-class Kingdom anointing. Don't let anyone tell you otherwise.

⇨ Entrepreneurship is one of the best opportunities to exercise the Kingdom mandate that God gave to Adam.

⇨ The core principles of what many would consider business best practices can be found in the Bible. Therefore, it just makes sense for us to utilize the Bible to help shape our business ideas and activities.

⇨ If you have a dream to be in business it came from God - what I like to call a God-idea - and He will empower you to succeed.

⇨ Just because you are a Christian does not mean you are guaranteed success in business. You must still operate with diligence in obedience and excellence using sound business principles.

⇨ As a Kingdom CEO the Holy Spirit gives you a significant competitive advantage in the marketplace. Therefore, strategic planning is a spiritual activity when He directs it.

⇨ Every Kingdom entrepreneur's business is a ministry. The marketplace presents perfect opportunities to invite and disciple people into God's family. However, you must seek direction from the Holy Spirit to determine exactly how he wants your business to function in that role because every business is different.

⇨ Kingdom entrepreneurship is similar to social entrepreneurship in that the focus is on more than just financial profits. There is an additional focus on how the business impacts people, the communities in which they live, and the issues that affect them.

⇨ Are you too busy pursuing your business instead of God's? We have the responsibility and privilege to invite people to the Kings' feast. We can't be satisfied that we are already at the table (Matthew 4).

⇨ Our influence for the Kingdom comes from our reputation (integrity) in the marketplace.

⇨ We must leverage where we are to help people see the love and power of Jesus to change their lives.

It's time to incorporate the Kingdom into your dream, into your business, and into your life... *Let's go!*

* * * * *

"Now is the accepted time, not tomorrow, not some more convenient season. It is today that our best work can be done and not some future day or future year. It is today that we fit ourselves for the greater usefulness of tomorrow. Today is the seed time, now are the hours of work, and tomorrow comes the harvest and the playtime."
~W.E.B. DuBois

* * * * *

PAUL WILSON, JR.

SECTION 1

THINK IT!

CHAPTER 1

THE ENTREPRENEURIAL MIND OF CHRIST

"Let this mind be in you, which was also in Christ Jesus."
Philippians 2:5 (KJV)

Cultivating the Entrepreneurial Mind of Christ

Albert Einstein was an intellectual phenomenon. Steve Jobs was a creative mastermind. Thomas Edison was a genius as bright as they come (pun intended). However none of these entrepreneurial inventors measures up to the brilliance, inventiveness, resourcefulness, prowess, and many other words I could use to describe our indescribable God.

God is the original and ultimate entrepreneur. In the beginning of Genesis 1, through Jesus (Hebrews 1:2), He created something incredible out of chaos. At the end of Genesis 1, they created man and woman in their divine image and told them to take dominion over the earth, be fruitful, and multiply. In order for us to accomplish these three mandates we have to use divine characteristics of entrepreneurship, including but not limited to faith, intelligence, creative ability, and resourcefulness, all of which God displayed as He manifested the universe.

The most widely accepted definition of entrepreneurship was coined more than thirty-five years ago by Harvard Business School professor Howard Stevenson. He defined it as *"The pursuit of opportunity without regard to resources currently controlled."* This definitely describes God's approach to creation, but with a major exception. He definitely pursued the opportunity to "invent" the earth and mankind, but He wasn't worried about resources, knowing He controls all of them anyway.

When most people hear the word entrepreneur they automatically think about business and selling stuff. However, you don't have to be in business to be entrepreneurial. My simple definition for being entrepreneurial is the ability to create value for people using attributes given to us by God. So using this definition, everyone should be entrepreneurial, which also describes how we should be operating in the world with the mind of Christ.

* * * * *

"The eyes of the Kingdom change everything."
~Lance Wallnau

* * * * *

Let's discuss some of the many characteristics of successful entrepreneurs and how they relate to operating effectively with the mind of Christ in the kingdom of God.

Faith

God spoke the world into existence, but He first had to believe that His words had creative power. Hebrews 11:6 says it is impossible to please God without faith. Similarly, it is nearly impossible to be entrepreneurial without strongly believing in yourself and in the ideas that you have. Accomplishing anything significant for God requires the constant application of your faith. God believed in Himself when He created the universe. You must believe in Him to accomplish the assignments He gives you.

Vision

Vision works closely with faith. Vision gives us a clear mental picture of what we need to have faith for. We are instructed by Habakkuk 2:2 to write the vision and make it plain. And we know from Proverbs 29:18 that without a vision the people perish. We need vision, because it gives us a hopeful expectation of something different or better than what we currently see. Fortunately, God's vision for your life is even bigger than yours. One of my favorite quotes is by D.L. Moody, who made a significant statement about vision: *"We must dream, because we were created in the image of the One who sees things that are not and wills them to be."*

Integrity

God is the same yesterday, today, and forever (Hebrews 13:8). His character never changes like shifting shadows (James 1:17). It is impossible for Him to lie (Hebrews 6:18) and His word always comes true (Isaiah 55:11). One of the main reasons Jesus got angry in the temple, threw out the businesspeople, and called them thieves is not because they were doing business. It is because they were doing business dishonestly! Always do right. And always do what you say and say what you do. Under-promise and over-deliver. You will not be in business very long if your word cannot be trusted. Always remember, do not let your charisma take you places where your character cannot keep you there, because a good name is worth far more than great riches (Proverbs 22:1).

Purpose

True entrepreneurs are not just out to make a buck. They want to be part of something bigger than themselves, i.e. revolutionary ideas, changing lives, new inventions, fresh innovations, etc. God gives life to purpose and purpose to life. He was not random or haphazard in what He did at the genesis of the world. He wanted to do something that had never been done before – design a new being with whom He could demonstrate the immensity of His love. He was so purposeful that He already had a plan in place when Adam messed up the perfect set up (John 3:16). Purpose should proceed all of your planning. For those in business, why are you in business? For those considering making the jump, why do you aspire to be an entrepreneur? Your motivation for business should have everything to do with why God created you.

Intelligence

Entrepreneurs do not always get the best grades in school, but they are usually very bright in that they constantly use their brains think through problems, issues, and opportunities. Unfortunately, some Christians think that their intellect is no longer needed once they commit their lives to Christ. The total opposite is true. When we get saved, we are to stop thinking, but we must commit all of our minds to Christ and allow him to transform how we think and what we think about (Romans 12:2). When we think like he thinks we will be able to tap into an eternal knowledge base that surpasses all human understanding. In Christ is hidden all the treasures of wisdom and knowledge (Colossians 2:3). So if you need a business idea, ask the One who has all the ideas.

Creativity

This one goes right along with intelligence. To see a simple example of God's creativity, just take a walk outside and look at how many different types of plants, trees, and flowers He made. Botanists estimate that there are more than 10,000 species of flowering plants. Jesus also sets a great example of using his divine creativity. If you look at all of his miracles, very seldom do you see him performing duplicates. John mused that all the miracles Jesus did could not be contained in all the books in the world (John 21:25). No doubt there was a lot of creative juices flowing during his life. Having the mind of Christ – powered by the Holy Spirit - gives you a competitive advantage over others without him. John 14:26 states that the Holy Spirit will teach us all things, so you can best believe he will reveal witty ideas to you that no one has ever thought of (1 Corinthians 2:9). How are you exercising your creative juices?

Talents & Gifts

We know that God is all-powerful and has no lack of ability to get things done. What's also true is that He gave every person a unique set of talents, abilities, gifts, and skills. He expects you to use – and improve – what you have been given (Matthew 25:23). Entrepreneurial people are excellent at using their talents intelligently and creatively to produce value. Do you know what special talents and abilities you have? How are you using them intelligently and creatively?

Perseverance

Life can be very challenging and so can business. God knows this firsthand. He faithfully endures through His creation's blatant rebellion, even after He freely gave them His most valuable possession. Jesus had to persevere through a tortuous trial and execution in order to fulfill his purpose. Perseverance involves a great deal of stick-to-it-ness, resourcefulness, and a never-say-quit attitude in the face of seemingly overwhelming obstacles. It takes a persevering mindset to endure what he did and still come out as the champion. Jesus expects us not to just look at his example, but to also follow it as we face trials of many kinds.

Patience

Patience is a close brother of perseverance. Delayed gratification is an invaluable asset. You have to be confident that *"your vision is yet for the appointed time; it hastens toward the goal and it will not fail. Though it tarries, wait for it; For it will certainly come, it will not delay"* (Habakkuk 2:3, NASB). God is patient with us, because He sees our end from our beginning (Isaiah 46:10), and He knows greater things are in store for us than what we may be currently experiencing (Jeremiah 29:11). Entrepreneurs are intimately acquainted with the principle of Seed, Time, and Harvest. They realize that a proper investment now of their time, talents, and treasures, will yield a profitable return in due season. Patience allows you not make hasty decisions. And while you are waiting for certain things to happen you are still planting more seeds.

Follow-through (vs. procrastination)

God's plans His work and then works His plans. He does not wait when He's supposed to be working. He does not delay when He's supposed to be doing. He is perfect love, so He has no fear to keep Him from moving forward. Entrepreneurially minded people take action more than they take breaks. Even in the times when it seemed like Jesus was delaying, he was very purposeful in his actions. If you already have the vision and the permission from God, what are you waiting for?

Courage

Courage turns your faith in action. Courage is often associated with taking risks. Interestingly, God took a risk creating human beings with the free will to reject Him. God took a risk creating a ransom plan by sending His son Jesus to redeem those who rejected Him. God takes a risk every day by allowing people to call themselves Christ-followers, even though we do not always do what Jesus did and say what he said. God is courageous, so He did not give us a spirit of fear, but a spirit of power, love, and a sound mind (2 Timothy 1:7), which we are to use to bring the realities of heaven down to earth.

Solutions-driven

Entrepreneurial people spend the majority of their time solving problems, generating value, and fostering positive change for themselves and others. They do not entertain pity parties. They waste little time complaining about things they either have no power over or are not intending on doing something about. They are all about blessing others through the intelligent and creative application of their time, talents, and treasures. They do not withhold good from people, because they realize it is in their power to do good for them (Proverbs 3:27), which is what the true Gospel of Jesus looks like in action (James 1:27). God sent Jesus as the #1 solution for our problems. How are you using Jesus to solve the world's problem?

Hopefully it is easy for you to see how Jesus exercised each of these entrepreneurial characteristics while he lived on the earth. Therefore, if we want to be like Christ, we must embrace the mind of Christ (1 Corinthians 2:16), which was very much entrepreneurial.

In order to bring the Kingdom of God from heaven down to earth in a literal sense, we must utilize Holy Spirit-inspired entrepreneurial ideas to do good works, by turning spiritual truths into practical, holistic solutions that bring real, positive, lasting change to people's lives. That is when the world will really see our lights shine and glorify God in heaven!

* * * * *

"Some men see things as they are and ask why. Others dream of things that never were and ask why not."
~G.B. Shaw

* * * * *

CHAPTER 2

MY IDENTITY VS. MY IMAGE

"God said to Moses, "I am who I am." And he said, "Say this to the people of Israel, 'I am has sent me to you.'"
Exodus 3:14

Affirming Your Life Purpose

The calling to business is just as significant and relevant to the Body of Christ as the call to pastor or be a missionary. You are just as anointed as those called into pulpit ministry. This is why our journey begins with an exploration of your life purpose prior to us delving into the business planning process. The truth is you are God's business and He wants you to know what your purpose is so that you can operate fully in it as you operate your business.

In the next few chapters I will take you through some exercises that will either help you affirm some things about your purpose that you already knew and discover some things about your purpose that you may not have known. If you want to go deeper in understanding your life purpose, please read my first book *Dream B.I.G. in 3D: How to Pursue a Bold, Innovative, God-inspired Life!* This is the source of these exercises and much more.

Who are you?

In our society we often confuse identity and image. Your identity is how you define yourself in a way that transcends your relationships, job, and other things that inadequately or incompletely describe you. It's the person God originally designed you to be. Your identity is the foundation of your life. Without a strong understanding of your identity, you will compromise when difficult challenges come to you.

On the other hand, your image is who you want everyone else to think you are. There's nothing wrong with focusing on having a positive image... if it is a true reflection of your identity. The problem is that most people we encounter today in life and in the media are false images. They spend more time working on their image (outward appearance) rather than developing their identity (internal character). After a while, if no attention is paid to the foundation the whole structure will begin to crumble.

Be vs. Do

Standard Definition Living

Do-Have-Be = "I am my profession."

Do	Have	Be
Study medicine	Degree	Doctor
Police academy	Badge, gun	Police officer
Sing	Record deal	Professional musician
American dream	Money, home, cars	Successful

High Definition Living
Be-Do-Have: "My identity determines my do."

Be	Do	Have
Knowledge facilitator	Teach, consult, coach	
Entrepreneur	Operate business, non-profit	Fulfillment in others' success Wealth for self and others Student transformation Influence, changed lives
Encourager	Inspire others (writing, speaking, singing, other)	
Leader	Pastor, politician, CEO	

〈〈〈❖〉〉〉

B.I.G. Idea:
You don't stop BEING just because your situation changes.

〈〈〈❖〉〉〉

When you have an accurate picture of your identity, you understand that your true value/worth is not tied to a job or career path. Your Creator has determined your worth and has given you the ability and opportunity to choose different paths within His purpose for your life.

Don't allow yourself to be pigeonholed into pursuing a single job or career path. You have more inside of you than that. Figure out what your "be" is then identify the different ways in which you can live it out to your full potential. Just prepare to be flexible and understand that our plans may not be the same as God's.

Let's move forward and figure out how to find our "be." It starts with your C.O.R.E. Identity.

Discover Your C.O.R.E. Identity
Just like the mighty oak tree started out as a small, simple, indistinguishable seed, at the core of who you are is the seed of your potential. Within the properties of the oak tree's seed resides all the essential traits necessary to grow a strong, healthy tree.

Residing within you also are all the essential elements needed to live a bold, innovative, God-inspired life. What you have to do is nurture and care for the seed of your potential in order to fulfill your potential. Let's dig a little deeper to see what's inside your C.O.R.E.

C.O.R.E. Elements
> ⇨ **Character**: Your commitment to a standard of values that determine your internal capacity to handle responsibility morally and ethically.
> ⇨ **Outlook**: Your vision for an ideal future that allows you to have a deep concern for a particular societal issue.
> ⇨ **Relationships**: The specific groups of people that are directly or indirectly impacted by the issues that I care most about.
> ⇨ **Energy**: The motivating factors that get you excited to do what you do best to make a difference with people and issues.

C.O.R.E. Questions
Asking yourself these questions will help you to determine what your answers are for each of the C.O.R.E. identity elements.
> ⇨ **Character:** Who do I want to become?

> ⇨ **Outlook**: What is my vision for the future?

> ⇨ **Relationships**: Whom do I want to impact?

> ⇨ **Energy**: What do I love to do that I can use to make a difference?

C.O.R.E. Values

Values are principles, standards, or qualities on which a person bases their beliefs. They help to define your identity. They also serve as boundaries for your life, because your values influence your choices. With a river, boundaries help to keep the force and energy of the water moving in a certain direction. Water without boundaries becomes like a swamp - stagnant, smelly, and devoid of healthy life. Values help you to channel your potential in a positive, productive, and prosperous direction.

Even if you haven't written them down, you make choices everyday that are based on your values. It is extremely important that you write down your values, because they help you prepare in advance to know when to say "yes" and when to say "no". Examples of values include: honesty, integrity, loyalty, and purity, along with many others.

What are your C.O.R.E. values?

1) _____

2) _____

3) _____

4) _____

5) _____

6) _____

7) _____

My C.O.R.E. Purpose Statement

Your C.O.R.E. purpose statement summarizes your life mission and provides direction and motivation for your life and career decisions. This statement incorporates your C.O.R.E. values and identity elements. And just like your values, it will help you to know which career path to say "yes" or "no" to. Specific ways in which a well-defined purpose statement include:

✓ **Compass**: Provides general direction for your life pathway.
✓ **Benchmark**: Anchor point that operates as a measurement standard to gauge your progress toward your goals and dreams.

《《❖》》

B.I.G. Idea:
Keep your vision in front of you, so that you will keep going even when you get discouraged.

《《❖》》

Purpose Statement Model:
"I am a _____ (describe character),   who   will _____(outlook   for   the future) for _____ (target group,   i.e.   family,   community,   youth)   by/through _____ (energy)."

Example #1:
"I am an enthusiastic encourager (C) who will bring a positive life perspective (O) to everyone I meet (R) by writing inspiring poems and songs (E)."

Example #2:
"I am an entrepreneurial leader (C) who will develop solutions to eradicate poverty (O) for communities and families in Africa (R) through entrepreneurial ventures (E)."

Writing two or three of these statement about yourself will help you to craft an inspiring theme for your life story, possibly before you have even lived it.

1)

2)

3)

⟨⟨⟨❖⟩⟩⟩

B.I.G. Idea:
Your ultimate fulfillment will be found in who you are to become, not what
you hope to achieve or accumulate!

⟨⟨⟨❖⟩⟩⟩

CHAPTER 3

DEFINING MY DREAMSCOPE

"And it shall come to pass afterward, that I will pour out my Spirit on all flesh; your sons and your daughters shall prophesy, your old men shall dream dreams, and your young men shall see visions."
Joel 2:28

What is a DreamScope?

So much of our lives are spent working, it does not make sense to me that God considers it a waste of time what we do during the proverbial 9 to 5 window of each day. Therefore, in all that we do we should work as unto the Lord and not unto people (Colossians 3:23). Furthermore, our work should be enjoyable, not toilsome and laborious (Ecclesiastes 5:18-20), because we are no longer under the curse of work as a result of Adam's sin (Galatians 3:13). Our work should also be financially beneficial (3 John 1:2).

Most people settle below the life God has for them, especially as it relates to their work life, because unfortunately they do not believe it is possible to find work they enjoy, that they are good at, and can support their lifestyle financially. Others just do not understand how to bring together their personality, passions, and skills to create a dream business or career that provides spiritual, professional, and financial fulfillment. This is precisely what we are going to show you, so that you can experience more of what God has prepared for you in this life (John 10:10).

⟨⟨⟨❖⟩⟩⟩

B.I.G. Idea:
God has already planned a place for you to prosper!

⟨⟨⟨❖⟩⟩⟩

You can think of the DreamScope as a combination of a microscope and a telescope, designed not for scientific discoveries, but life discoveries. The purpose of a microscope is to magnify objects that are too small to be seen by the naked or unaided eye. So your DreamScope helps you to examine some critical details of your life to magnify unique patterns and special strengths. The purpose of a telescope is to detect and observe distant objects. So your DreamScope will help you to discover unknown internal territories that are yet to be explored. These magnified and newly discovered territories, which represent unnoticed, disregarded, or neglected motivations/desires, need to be studied and thoroughly considered, because they could be revealing windows for you to see how to fulfill your life dreams.

⟨⟨⟨❖⟩⟩⟩

B.I.G. Idea:
Never underestimate the power of a dream submitted to God!

⟨⟨⟨❖⟩⟩⟩

This powerful DreamScope tool will equip you to begin bringing congruency and alignment between who you are, what you desire, and what you are best equipped and suited to do. It will also help you determine your uniquely designed life pathway that best aligns and propels your life forward.

"My DreamScope"

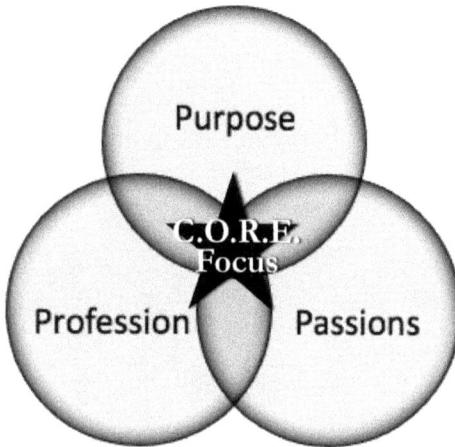

The three components of this tool are your 1) purpose, 2) passions, and 3) profession. Your purpose circle represents the specific calling or direction for your life. Your passions circle represents your intense desire or enthusiasm related to a particular activity or cause. Your profession circle represents your career or educational path that will allow you to make money in the marketplace using acquired knowledge and skills. The C.O.R.E. Focus area in the middle is where each of these three critical components of your life intersect, allowing you to identify a strategic pathway for your life.

Completing the activities below will help you begin to strategically align your desires with His will.

Purpose: The specific calling or assignment for your life.
    Key Questions:
    ⇨ Who are you inspired to be?
    ⇨ What do you feel you were created to do?
    ⇨ What problem do you want to solve?
    ⇨ What do you see a need for?

⇨ What do you want to be known for?
⇨ What legacy do you want to create?

Writing Activity: Write down your thoughts related to these questions. You can use your answers to the C.O.R.E. questions as a reference.

Passions: Your intense desire or enthusiasm related to a particular activity or cause.

Key Questions:
⇨ What gets you excited?
⇨ What issues motivate you to take action?
⇨ What irritates you?
⇨ What do you daydream about?
⇨ What do you always talk about?
⇨ What would you do for free?
⇨ What are you willing to suffer or die for?

Writing Activity: Write down your thoughts related to these questions. You can use your answers to the C.O.R.E. questions as a reference.

Profession: Your career or educational path that will allow you to reap financial rewards in the marketplace in exchange for applying your acquired knowledge and skills.

Key Questions:

⇨ What are you really good at?

⇨ What area is your "10"?

⇨ In what ways are you unique from other people?

⇨ What do you get compliments on?

⇨ How are you first, best, or different?

Writing Activity: Write down your thoughts related to these questions. You can use your answers to the C.O.R.E. questions as a reference.

One key aspect of this Professional Skills component is its direct influence on your earning potential. Your ability to make money (and lots of it) is directly connected to how much value you can provide to a company or customers. What you are able to command (salary/wages) or charge (business pricing) is directly related to your ability to define and communicate your distinct value to potential customers.

When you go to a store to purchase an item, you are able to identify its value - what you have to pay for it - by the price tag on the item. Although you may disagree with the price on the tag, if you really want that item, you will pay for it. Likewise, your personal price T.A.G.S., which equate to your temperament, abilities, gifts, and significant experiences, determine your value in the marketplace. Read below to learn more about these incredibly valuable assets that you possess.

T.A.G.S. Assets:
⇨ **Temperament**: Work style and personality.
⇨ **Abilities**: Learned skills through education, practice, or experience.
⇨ **Gifts**: Abilities that seem to come naturally without much effort or practice.
⇨ **Significant Experiences**: Knowledge and work history.

Each area of T.A.G.S. can be considered a personal asset that has a specific value. All of your personal assets combined will determine your total value in the marketplace. The more defined and developed your T.A.G.S. the greater demand that you have. The more robust, and dynamic that your T.A.G.S. are, the more that you can command in salary (employee) or prices (entrepreneur). You will give yourself an incredible competitive advantage the more time, energy, and resources that you invest in understanding and enhancing your T.A.G.S.

<<<❖>>>

B.I.G. Idea:
You can determine your value in the marketplace when you accurately inventory and appraise your T.A.G.S.

<<<❖>>>

Writing Activity: You have to know your value before you can communicate it effectively to other people. Write down your personal assets within each area.

⇨ **Temperament (Work Style)**: Describe your personality by answering the following questions: Would you rather work on a team or alone? Would you rather work with people or with processes? Do you enjoy fast paced or slow paced work environments? Are you a maintainer or an innovator? Would you rather lead or follow?

⇨ **Abilities (Learned Skills)**: Describe your abilities by answering the following questions: What are your strengths? What skills have you learned or developed during your professional career or in your life?

⇨ **Gifts (Natural Talents)**: Describe your gifts by answering the following questions: What comes natural to you that does not require much practice? What are you able to do very easily that others struggle with?

⇨ **Significant Experiences (Knowledge and Work History):** Describe your significant experiences by answering the following questions: List 5 to 8 of the most significant personal, work, and/or educational experiences and what you learned from them. How can those experiences add value to others?

If you are having trouble completing these inventories, one thing that may help you is to write down all of your daily activities and determine which circles into which they fall. Doing it like this will also help you to see whether you are spending your time purposefully.

I will show you how to merge these circles and look for patterns that will help you to determine your C.O.R.E. Focus.

C.O.R.E. Focus

The goal of making the purpose, passion, and profession lists is to begin to identify characteristics of your life in each of three circles that are linked to things in the other circles. The middle area of the DreamScope where you find these linkages circles is your C.O.R.E. Focus. This area will highlight certain aspects of your life to which you should channel your focus for further exploration. Some key characteristics about your C.O.R.E. Focus include:

- ✓ Increases clarity for your C.O.R.E. Purpose Statement.
- ✓ Can add specificity to your C.O.R.E. Purpose Statement.
- ✓ Intersections reveal needed focus for exploration or experimentation.
- ✓ No natural intersections reveal opportunities for further self-examination.
- ✓ Helps identify areas of imbalance or neglect between these key components of your life.

C.O.R.E. Focus Exercise: Get a blank sheet of paper. Draw three big circles that overlap each other in the middle. Write one of the words purpose, passions, and professions in each of the circles. Go back to the lists that you wrote earlier and copy those respective lists into the appropriate circle. The common area in the middle of the circles represents the activities and interests of your life that have common threads. Begin to assess the connections and interactions between your lists.

Remember, the DreamScope is both a microscope (to help you magnify current patterns) and a telescope (to discover new possibilities for your life). The key takeaway from this exercise is that the activities or interests that cross over into the middle of all three circles are likely the things on which you need to start intentionally focusing more time, attention, and resources. Hopefully, you will begin to see some themes and patterns emerge from what you have written. Let's look at an example.

C.O.R.E. Focus Example

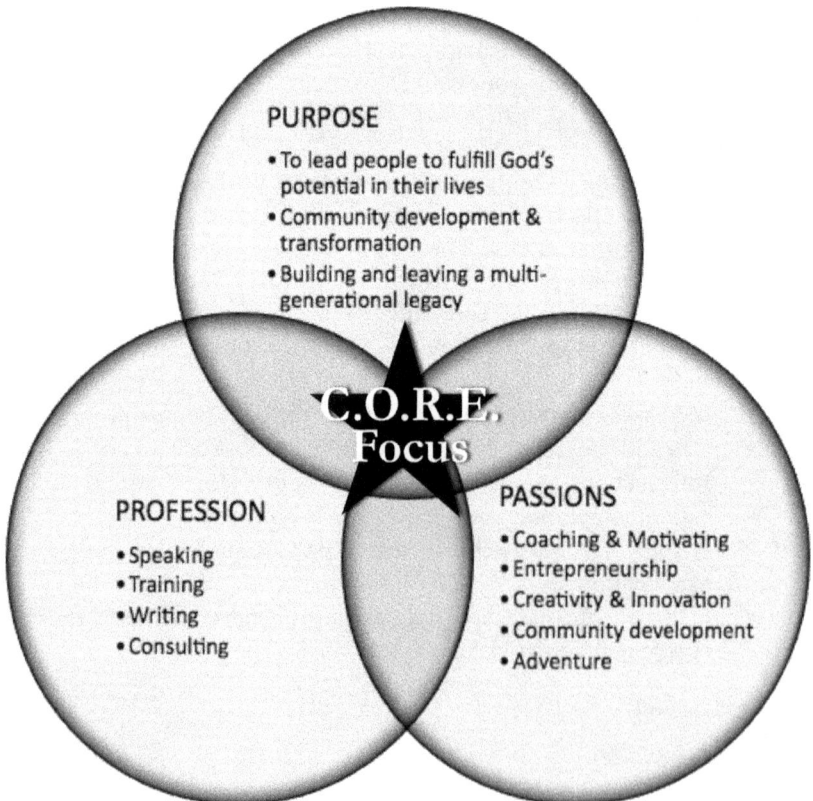

PURPOSE
- To lead people to fulfill God's potential in their lives
- Community development & transformation
- Building and leaving a multi-generational legacy

C.O.R.E. Focus

PROFESSION
- Speaking
- Training
- Writing
- Consulting

PASSIONS
- Coaching & Motivating
- Entrepreneurship
- Creativity & Innovation
- Community development
- Adventure

Three themes that emerge from this DreamScope example include:
1) Strong desire to motivate people through, coaching, speaking, training, writing.
2) Deep interest in businesses that relate to motivating people to fulfill their potential.
3) Serious inclination to focus on businesses that create opportunities to transform communities and build a legacy.

One thing I love about this tool is that as you move forward in your life, you can assess the opportunities that come your way to see if they align with your three circles. If they align with all three, it's probably a good indicator it's something you should seriously consider. The decision you may have to make at that point would be based on if it were the right timing. On the other hand, if new opportunities don't align with all three, it may not be something you want to engage, because it could move you away from optimally fulfilling your B.I.G. dreams.

⟪⟪❖⟫⟫

B.I.G. Idea:
You will be most fulfilled in your life when you are able to apply as much of your time, talents, energy, and resources as possible to your C.O.R.E. Focus.

⟪⟪❖⟫⟫

As a way to see how accurate you were with this exercise, compare your C.O.R.E. Focus to your C.O.R.E. Purpose Statement to see how closely aligned they are. If they are closely connected, you will know that you are on the right track. If they are going in totally opposite directions, you will need to take some more time for further self-examination and go through these assessments again.

CHAPTER 4

ANSWERING MY KINGDOM CALLING

"Therefore, brothers, be all the more diligent to confirm your calling and
election, for if you practice these qualities you will never fall."
2 Peter 1:10

What is a Vocation?

In today's society the concept of vocation has lost much of its original meaning. Most people connect the word vocation to having a job. Interestingly, it originated in the 15th century from the Latin word, *vocatio*, which means summons or to call. So the essence of this word vocation is not a job, but a calling. Therefore, you should not look at the business God has called you to build as just the work you do. You should look at it as your God-given calling within His Kingdom.

There is no such thing as sacred and secular within the Kingdom of God. Work is sacred, just like what would be considered traditional ministry is sacred. Being a secretary is as sacred as being a pastor. Being an entrepreneur is just as sacred as being a prophet. When you understand working in all you do as unto the Lord, you come to the realization that anything you do for God is sacred. And although there are many different gifts, offices, and roles within the Body of Christ, each one of them is needed and necessary to bring the manifestation of God's Kingdom to the earth.

Further, while a different anointing is needed to minister effectively from the pulpit versus ministering effectively in the marketplace, one is no more valuable than the other. They are just different. You are the church whenever and wherever you do business, which means you are in full-time ministry whether you knew it or not.

So stay in your lane. Don't feel pressured to pursue a pulpit in order to find significance in the Kingdom. You don't have to feel like a second-class Kingdom citizen if God didn't call you to operate in a church ministry position. God has positioned you right where He wants to get His greatest glory out of you.

* * * * *

"To live outside of God's will put us in danger;
to live in His will makes us dangerous."
~Erwin McManus

* * * * *

The Whole is Greater than the Parts

God has plans for you to thrive as a Kingdom entrepreneur, not just survive. And as we discussed in the previous chapter, you will thrive only to the extent that you have a close alignment of your purpose, passions, and professional skills. Let's take a look at what happens when you don't have a C.O.R.E. Focus and all three components are not considered equally as you are pursuing the activation of your purpose in the marketplace.

Single Dimension Focus

⇨ **Purpose Only Focus**: If a person is only focused on their purpose at the expense of the other two areas, they often settle for working out of a sense of duty or obligation. And because they believe this opportunity is connected to their purpose, but does not involve the other two spheres, this will usually lead to volunteer type work. There is nothing wrong with this if you want to keep it at that level, but if you want to earn a living connected to your purpose you have to broaden your perspective.

**PURPOSE=
Dutiful
Activity**

⇨ **Passion Only Focus**: You will hear many people say just follow your passion and you can have the career or business of your dreams. The reality is that this is not the whole picture. Just because you are passionate about something does not mean you can automatically turn it into a career or business. If you have no skill in that area or if God has not called you to that area then you should not be doing it. I really love music, but I have minimal musical skill. Further, God did not call me to the music industry. Therefore, I enjoy music as a hobby, but not as a profession.

**PASSION =
Hobby or
Interest**

⇨ **Professional Skills Only Focus**: This one is probably the most challenging areas of the three for most people, because you may be good at something professionally and have performed successfully for many years, but you are not passionate about this type of work, nor do you feel God has called you to work in this area long-term. I believe this mindset is a reflection of the unspoken disappointment and lack of fulfillment most people experience in the workplace today. Your purpose and passions are pointing you down a different path than the one that you are on right now, but you feel trapped because what you sense in your heart looks a lot different than where you are in your career right now.

Dual Dimension Focus

⇨ **Purpose + Passion**: Similar to the previous points that focused solely on purpose and passion, you can pursue opportunities that combine these areas, but you may not be able to receive adequate financial compensation if you do not have the professional skills that match what these opportunities require. So you may become a great advocate through your activities, but it may be very difficult to establish income that is sustainable.

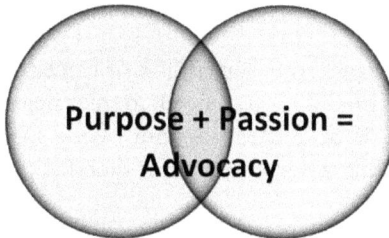

⇨ **Passion + Professional Skills**: Many people are good at what they do and are passionate about their work. In this scenario the only thing missing is a disconnection from their life purpose. This type of person may have a long profitable career, but there will still be a lack of fulfillment that may not surface until later in their professional life. Again, this person may find a way to fulfill their purpose outside of work, so this is not an indictment of their career choice.

Professional Skills + Passion = Career

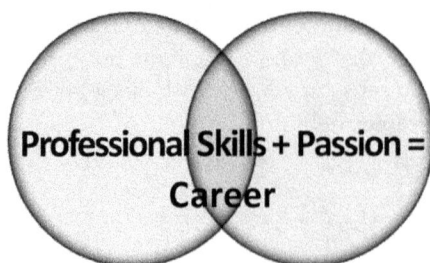

⇨ **Purpose + Professional Skills**: This path is similar to the previous one. You can be very successful if this is how you are positioned in your work life. However, what now may be meaningful and profitable could eventually become mundane and burdensome, resulting in frustration.

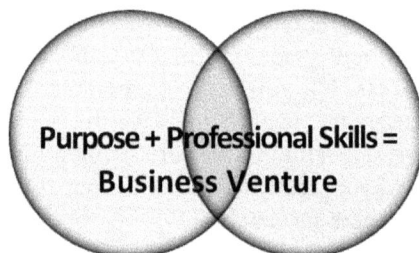

Purpose + Professional Skills = Business Venture

Take some time to assess your current job or career situation. Does it fit one of these six scenarios? Do you need to reevaluate where you have placed your priorities as it relates to your work life? If you are not completely fulfilled in what you are doing is it time for a change?

Kingdom Business Building Blocks

An enterprise that is created and operated as a Kingdom driven business should be an extension or expression of one's life mission. This ensures that you are not pursuing a business opportunity that is outside of God's purpose for your life. Even if the business is financially profitable, chasing what seems good may lead to unforeseen challenges, frustration, and ultimately a lack of fulfillment. A successful Kingdom entrepreneur is able to find close alignment between his/her life purpose and a profitable Kingdom business model.

Just like you discovered a C.O.R.E. Focus for your personal life, a profitable Kingdom business model has one also, deriving from your business's Culture, Outlook, Relationships, and Energy. The C.O.R.E. Focus of your business is established when you are able to identify a business idea that integrates three key characteristics that leverage one another: 1) Real Needs, 2) Relationships, and 3) Revenues. Let's take a closer look at each of these three:

1) **Real Needs**: Your product/service meets a specific need, solves a problem, or satisfies a desire in the marketplace.
   - ✓ Is your idea directly answer a consumer need or desire?
   - ✓ Will you be first, best, or different?
   - ✓ Is there a gap between needs and current solutions?
   - ✓ Are there any alternatives?
   - ✓ What is the performance of current alternatives?

2) **Relationships**: There are specific groups of people God is expecting you to impact who are connected to what you are offering.
   - ✓ Customers
   - ✓ Employees
   - ✓ Partners
   - ✓ Suppliers
   - ✓ Financiers
   - ✓ Advisors
   - ✓ Community stakeholders

3) **Revenues**: Your idea is marketable and able to generate sustainable revenues.
   - ✓ What is the market potential?
   - ✓ Are people willing to pay for it?
   - ✓ Do similar products/services currently exist that would limit your market potential?
   - ✓ Is this a fad or does it have long-term potential?
   - ✓ Who is the competition?

Each of these individual building blocks has its strengths and advantages. However, if any of three areas are out of balance or not functioning well your business will not thrive. For example if you have identified a need in the marketplace, but you do not have a profit-making revenue model to deliver the solution to customers you will not be in business very long. Likewise, if you are great at building relationships, but you have not identified a product or service that meets a specific need or desire in the marketplace you will not produce any cash flow. Another example is you can have a great product that everybody wants with a price that generates great revenues, but if your customer service is terrible eventually it will catch up to you and cost you customers and sales.

That is why I refer so much to balance and alignment between these areas. Your business is postured with a strong foundation and growth potential when you are able to focus time and energy on making sure all three components are functioning properly together.

* * * * *

"Build a business that brings you an abundance of passion, purpose, and profits! A business that makes nothing but money is a poor business."
~Henry Ford

* * * * *

The Best of Both Worlds

It is possible to experience the best that heaven and earth have to offer. You can have a business that is successful by the world's standards, but that also glorifies God. When you are a Kingdom CEO walking in the fullness of your life purpose and your business is operating in its C.O.R.E. Focus you will begin to experience the best of both worlds. Take a look at how the two come together...

"Best of Both Worlds"

Meets a **REAL NEED** in the marketplace.

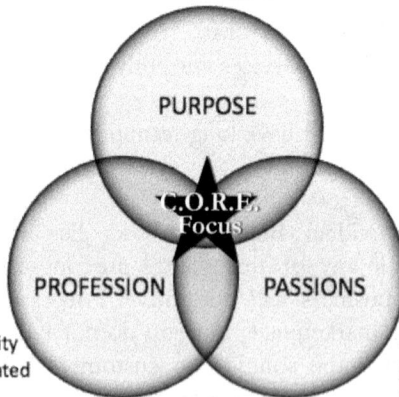

PURPOSE

C.O.R.E. Focus

PROFESSION   PASSIONS

REVENUES: Opportunity to be highly compensated for your expertise.

Opportunity to be build **RELATIONSHIPS** and impact many people.

When there is balance and efficient execution between your C.O.R.E. life purpose and your C.O.R.E. business model, you will experience great fulfillment — spiritually, professionally, and financially.

⟨⟨⟨❖⟩⟩⟩

B.I.G. Idea:
C.O.R.E. Focus Activation =
Spiritual + Professional + Financial Fulfillment

⟨⟨⟨❖⟩⟩⟩

Exercise: Describe how well your life purpose connects with your God-idea.

Exercise: Describe how well your life purpose is balanced with your business vision and what changes might need to be made.

CHAPTER 5

GOD IDEAS VS. GOOD IDEAS

"As it is written: What no eye has seen, what no ear has heard, and what no human mind has conceived the things God has prepared for those who love him, these are the things God has revealed to us by his Spirit. The Spirit searches all things, even the deep things of God."
1 Corinthians 2:9-11

Let There Be Light

In Genesis 1, before God broke up the chaos in the earth, the first thing He did was bring light to the atmosphere. This light dispelled the darkness and disorder, and began to bring order and organization to the earth.

God's light is the equivalent of revelation, illumination, and enlightenment. Chaos exists all around us in the marketplace and in our communities. His light awakens us from a stupor of confusion and misdirection (Ephesians 5:14). His light brightens the path of our walk with Him.

As it relates to your business, God's light is necessary for you to get fresh revelation and ideas to solve problems in businesses, schools, governments, communities, and anywhere else in the marketplace that He called you to create impact. However, if you don't first get a revelation from God about what's happening in those places you won't have the means to bring effective, long-term solutions to those problems.

Your ideas alone aren't good enough without God's engagement. If you don't have God's enlightenment infusing your ideas, you won't have what's needed to break through the chaos and confusion with that's oppressing people.

* * * * *

"Good is the enemy of great."
~Jim Collins

* * * * *

The Deception of Good Ideas

You have probably heard it said that good ideas are "a dime a dozen." It is really fairly easy to come up with a "good" idea for a business. However, while these ideas may seem good at the time of conception, they are not necessarily good for you. Why is that?

Every idea that comes to your mind is not meant for you to do. Moreover, ideas you see working for other people may not be meant for you to do. You must identify what God has called you to do and stick to that. Many Christians spend a lot of time dealing with trial and error in their businesses, because they don't take the time to get all the needed instructions from God. And while He redeems our time and experiences, some trials could be avoided and time could be saved by only doing what God has truly told us to do, not just allowed us to do.

Do you realize that having the mind of Christ is more than helping us think pure thoughts and make the right decisions? Although, these aspects are critical to a holy human life, they are not the only qualities of Christ's mind that were meant to benefit us here on the earth. Remember, this is the same mind that created this world and the entire universe. This mind was the conduit for amazing miracles. And this mind also provides a window into a glorious future. If you are an entrepreneur, it is especially important that you rethink your perspective on the practical possibilities of this amazing spiritual asset. Christ mind is not just good. It's perfect. James 1:17 tells us that *"Every good gift and every perfect gift is from above, coming down from the Father of lights…"*

One of the most beautiful things about the times we live in is that God's Spirit is being poured out in greater waves to produce dreamers and visionaries. This outpouring is producing a transfer of exclusive wisdom, knowledge, and ideas from heaven down to earth.

The question you must answer is did your "good" idea come from Christ's mind or your own?

Your Business is an Answer to Somebody's Prayer

If you are walking closely with God, the ideas that you have for your business don't originate from you. As Proverbs 8:12 instructs us, witty ideas and inventions come from God. He wants to use you and your business to bring solutions to your community, city, or industry that solve problems and change lives. Somebody is praying to God right now and needs what you have to offer. Don't take lightly the ideas that He gives you and cast them off as wayside seed (Mark 4:15). Their blessing and yours is dependent upon you receiving and obeying was God is telling you to do through your business.

In order to bring the Kingdom of God from Heaven down to earth in a literal sense, we must utilize Holy Spirit-inspired entrepreneurial ideas to do good works, by turning spiritual truths into practical, holistic solutions that bring real, positive, and lasting change to people's lives. That is when the world will really see our lights shine brightly and glorify God in heaven!

So the question is what darkness (confusion) is your business designed to bring light (revelation) to? What disorder is your business designed to bring peace to? How effectively you can answer these questions is directly connected to understanding your calling in business and generating value for which you are compensated extremely well.

* * * * *

"The idea that burns in your heart is the answer to someone's need. Do it.
God is not looking for someone important. He is looking for someone's
obedience."
~Dr. Deana Murphy

* * * * *

Biblical Examples of Entrepreneurial Ingenuity

Before we look ahead to your business ideas, let's first look back at
some Biblical examples of creative ideas God gave to people that helped to
facilitate His agenda getting accomplished here:

⇨ God gives Noah specific instructions on how to design and build a
boat when it had never even rained. (Genesis 6)

⇨ Isaac was a business maverick who went against conventional
thinking in the midst of a famine and grew his business and estate
exponentially. (Genesis 26)

⇨ Jacob used an innovative sheep-breeding concept that dramatically
increased his assets and wealth so he could divest from his uncle and
transition to managing his own estate. (Genesis 30-25-43)

⇨ Joseph utilized an excellent wealth and asset management plan before
and during a famine that saved Egypt from disaster and positioned it
to become an economic superpower that other nations would have
to rely on to survive. (Genesis 41)

⇨ God gave Moses a national relocation plan for 600,000 people.
(Exodus 3)

⇨ Moses received explicit, detailed instructions from God on how to
design and build the Tabernacle in the wilderness. (Exodus 25)

⇨ Joshua and his army used an unusual God-inspired military strategy
to destroy the city of Jericho. (Joshua 6)

⇨ Gideon used a human resource strategy to downsize his army from
30,000 to 300 men that eventually would defeat his enemies. (Judges
7)

⇨ Elisha helped a desperate widow launch an oil business that paid off
her debts and sustained her family. (2 Kings 4:1-7)

⇨ Daniel was a respected governmental advisor, strategic consultant,
and foreign affairs expert for four different kings. (Daniel)

⇨ Jesus helped the disciples exponentially grow their fishing business
when he told them to cast their net on the other side of the boat and
they caught more fish than they could handle alone. (Luke 5:1-11)

⇨ Jesus told Peter to get money to pay their taxes out of a fish's mouth. (Matthew 17:24-27)

⇨ Peter and the other Apostles implemented a community development strategy through organizational restructuring that more efficiently divided their responsibilities and significantly benefitted those in need. (Acts 6:1-7)

Here are four lessons we can take away from all of these examples:

1) Your goals should be bigger than money. You should have a much bigger vision in mind for your family and your community. You should be inspired by a goal that is greater than just your material possessions.

2) Supernatural doesn't mean spooky. God is supernatural, meaning He will give you ideas and strategies that supersede our natural or logical ways of thinking. Supernatural insights always have practical applications that produce exponential results. After you come down from the mountain with divine revelation get ready for the hands-on implementation.

3) Be willing to try new things outside of your prior experience and expertise. Although He can, God doesn't have to use your previous education, experience, or expertise to accomplish His goals through your life. Whether through divine impartation or discovery you can implement His strategy without reservation and obtain amazing outcomes.

4) Prosperity comes through the diligent application of godly principles. If these people never applied the ideas they never would have achieved those incredible results. Further, don't stop with one success. Continue the process as long as God leads you so you can keep reproducing success. Don't settle for good when God planned for you to be great!

* * * * *

"Expectation never looks for a place to settle…
The next level doesn't always look like the next level."
~ J. Calvin Tibbs

* * * * *

Modern Day Example: George Washington Carver Was a Spirit-Led Inventor

There are many modern day examples that we could look at to see how God similarly inspired businesspeople and other leaders with His ideas to impact the world. One of the best examples is George Washington Carver. This former slave overcame major obstacles and trials throughout his life to become one of the most prolific scientists and inventors the United States and the world has ever seen.

The following powerful synopsis of his life is from the blog, *League of Everyday Doxologists* :

Dr. Carver was an agricultural chemist and agronomist, who helped transform the agricultural industry. He was a scientist and a man of faith who was inspired by the Creator of the nature around him, which became the foundation for so many of his scientific discoveries.

Southern agriculture industry relied heavily upon cotton; however, this single crop depleted the soil. Dr. Carver discovered that alternative crops such as peanuts and soybeans could restore the fertility in the soil. In addition, to create demand for these crops, he developed over 300 products from peanuts, 118 products from sweet potatoes and over 500 dyes. By the 1940s, peanut had become the second largest crop in the South. In this way, Dr. Carver used his scientific expertise to transform an entire economy to help those in need.

Dr. Carver claimed he could not have done what he did without God's inspiration: *"God is going to reveal to us things He never revealed before if we put our hands in His...The method is revealed to me the moment I am inspired to create something new. Without God to draw aside the curtain I would be helpless."*

George Washington Carver also heeded well the Lord's command to serve others. He impacted generations of farmers by uncovering agricultural pearls that God enabled him to uncover. Doing scientific research for the glory of the Lord resulted in serving others with practical and inventive ways for using creation as it was designed to be used. (Source: League of Extraordinary Doxologists, http://www.doxologists.org/george-washington-carver-god-glorifying-agricultural-innovator/)

How to Define God Ideas

God doesn't need to use get-rich-quick schemes or gimmicks to bring wealth into your business. On the other hand, He will give you innovative ideas, keen insights, and witty inventions to create products or services that produce wealth. So let's define some criteria for what a God idea should look like:

1) **Providential**: It's connected to God's overall plan to advance His Kingdom on the planet.
2) **Partnership**: God often gives seemingly impossible opportunities that require His supernatural intervention and human help. It will also require a great deal of faith as you realize you are wholly

inadequate for the task. If you can do it by yourself without much faith needed, it did not come from Him.

3) **Purpose driven**: It's connected to your individual God-given purpose. Although they may be uncomfortable or unfamiliar, His ideas will not lead you into something that's outside of His ultimate plan for your life.

4) **People focused**: It's going to bless other people, not just benefit you. It may not have a Christian label on it, but it should be able to enhance your relational exposure and create opportunities for interactions.

5) **Practical**: It meets a real need or satisfies a desire that doesn't dishonor God. Although the source is supernatural, the application and implementation will be tangible. He's not going to give you an idea for a product or service that nobody needs or wants.

6) **Provision**: God's plans always come with provision, which means He will also give you the idea(s) for how to fund it. If you don't have clarity on that yet, it might not be time for you to move forward with it.

7) **Profitable**: The blessing of the Lord makes rich and He adds no sorrow with it (Proverbs 10:22). Your idea – with the right plan and execution – will have financial rewards connected to it. Further, you should be able to get it done without having to go into excessive debt, which would cause you sorrow instead of joy.

Many of you agreed with me up until the last point and then you got a little uneasy because I wrote that your God ideas should be financially profitable. Unfortunately, many Christians are in financial straits because they have rejected the idea that God creates ways for them to be financially prosperous. While money should never be your primary objective, without it you cannot build a sustainable, multi-generational enterprise that will bless more people than you can count.

God's Word says it rains on the just and the unjust (Matthew 5:45). One meaning of this scripture is that is He's always releasing ideas into the earthly realm through His Spirit. He's going to get them accomplished in the earth whether through Believers or unbelievers. It just makes sense that Christians should hear, obey, and reap the earthly and eternal rewards (while unbelievers only get the benefit of earthly rewards). Following spiritual principles always produces practical results. Don't allow God's ideas to become unprofitable wayside seeds in your life or business (Mark 4:4,15).

* * * * *

"If you are the seed of Abraham (and you are!), you have the DNA of an entrepreneur. You have the ability to create wealth....an anointing to create money out of nothing. Ideas pass right by you but if you're not in the right frequency because you're stressed, too busy, distracted...you will miss it."
~Shae Bynes

* * * * *

How to Generate God Ideas

It is the greatest honor to be asked by God to do something big for Him. Unfortunately, many Christians get the initial idea from God, but don't stick around long enough to get all the instructions on how to build the business, ministry, community organization, etc. The bigger the idea the more details He will need to give to ensure that it is successful and sustainable.

Prayer is the incubator of divine revelation, wisdom, and witty inventions. Our efforts to receive God's ideas will be multiplied when we rely more on the Spirit of God and less on our earthly abilities. This dependence will allow you to accelerate your success, reduce unnecessary trial and error, and shorten the gap between busyness and effectiveness.

《《❖》》

B.I.G. Idea:
Prayer is the incubator of divine revelation, wisdom, and witty inventions.

《《❖》》

One way to engage the Christ's mind for your business is to regularly go into prayer seeking instructions versus just having a list of requests. Your approach should be to ask, *"What do you want me to do?"* versus asking Him to bless your plan which He didn't initiate or that may not be best for you.

Of course when you do ask God for something related to your business, make sure you're not asking amiss (James 4:3). Come into agreement with His Word by asking for things you know He already wants to give you, such as wisdom (James 1), vision (Jeremiah 29:11), strategies (Isaiah 48:17), resources (Philippians 4:19), and insights to witty inventions (Proverbs 8:12). Therefore, you should always go into prayer seeking directions, not toting your list of requests or demands.

I would also encourage you to take Apostle Paul's advice in Ephesians 6:18, which was to *"pray in the Spirit on all occasions with all kinds of prayers and requests."* Dr. Carver did this all the time. Pray is your lifeline to God, so you should take advantage of this indispensable resource as often as you can. One of the major benefits of effectual and fervent pray is that you will receive insights and ideas that could only come from God. He wants you to prosper in your business, so it only makes sense that He would tell you how to do it.

Don't let prayer be like an emergency signal flare that you shoot up in the air when you're in trouble. Prayer should be your lifestyle that keeps you connected to the Source of the best ideas in the universe that money can't buy.

Here are some things to consider as you seek God for His ideas:

1) **Be Available**: Are you more interested in your plans or God's? This is a major factor in determining what He reveals to you.

2) **Be Attentive**: God downloads His ideas through various and sometimes unexpected sources, including prayer, visions/dreams, conversations, media, books, etc. Keep your natural and spiritual eyes open.

3) **Be Assertive**: God has not given you a spirit of fear, but of power, love, and a sound mind. Confidently expect God to do great things through you.

4) **Be Active**: Lazy hands bring poverty, but diligent hands produce wealth (Proverbs 10:4). Fresh God ideas often come as you're moving forward with what God has already shared with you. Move forward with the instructions you already have.

5) **Be Obedient**: Kingdom entrepreneurs are stewards of God's ideas meant for the earth. We must become doers of God's ideas!

Stay Connected to the Living Water

A tree can't grow without access to water. Your money won't grow without you accessing God's wisdom and power. The only way we can survive financial famines is to maintain an intimate relationship with the Spirit. This helps us develop the spiritual disciplines, endurance, and commitment needed to stay the course in life He established for us. These verses clearly show us the benefits of staying connected to God and the detriments if we don't:

"But his delight is in the law of the Lord, and on His law he meditates day and night. He shall be like a tree planted by streams of water, that yields its fruit in its season, and its leaf does not wither. In all that he does, he prospers." Psalm 1:2-3

"Blessed is the man who trusts in the LORD, whose trust is the LORD. He is like a tree planted by water, that sends out its roots by the stream, and does not fear when heat comes, for its leaves remain green, and is not anxious in the year of drought, for it does not cease to bear fruit." Jeremiah 17:7-8

Money grows where God flows. Proverbs 8 clearly tells us that from God gushes unmatched wisdom, which enables us to receive insights, ideas, and inventions that will yield financial benefits. Staying connected to Him guarantees growth and increase. He takes delight in blessing His children and you are the place on the planet where God wants to demonstrate the abundance of His love, which includes His ability and desire for you to have overflowing financial resources. Why? Because it will get people's attention when you can take care of not just your own needs, but also the needs of others. That absolutely will give you a platform to tell more people about Jesus.

<<<❖>>>

B.I.G. Idea:
Money grows where God flows.

<<<❖>>>

The key thing to remember in all this is what God reminded His family (and us) in Deuteronomy 8:18. God's ultimate purpose in giving us the power to get wealth is to establish His covenant on the planet. When you connect your desire for money to establishing God's Kingdom here by fulfilling the Great Commission, He is excited to bring increase to you, because He can trust you to use it the right way for His glory.

Build God's Business

God has a global agenda that He wants to accomplish and He wants to use you and your business to participate in this process. Therefore we must we must become doers of God's ideas. As such, you will have a special grace, anointing, and power to accomplish great exploits in business for His glory.

You could be one thought or idea away from a major business breakthrough. Just make sure you are building God's vision with His ideas in His strength.

SECTION II

INK IT!

CHAPTER 6

MY BUSINESS VISION, MISSION, & VALUES

"Write down the revelation and make it plain on tablets so that a herald
may run with it. For the revelation awaits an appointed time; it speaks of
the end and will not prove false."
Habakkuk 2:2-3

V-STAR BUSINESS PLANNING SYSTEM

Vision, Mission, & Values
What & Why?

Results
Measures?

C.O.R.E. Focus

Strategy
How?

Action Planning
What & When?

Target Market
Who?

Using Christ's Imagination

How would you like to always be in the right place at the right time making the right decisions? It most certainly can happen. It's called using the mind of Christ. The mind of Christ is the most valuable asset that you have as a Kingdom building entrepreneur.

Nevertheless, I'm convinced that the mind of Christ is the most underutilized resource within the Body of Christ. When we engage Christ's mind, we not only get his perspective on things, we also get access to all the treasures of wisdom and knowledge in the universe (Colossians 2:3). This wisdom was present when God established the foundations of the cosmos (Proverbs 8:27). Furthermore, His mind possesses the knowledge of witty inventions (Proverbs 8:12). Within his mind reside the deep things of God (1 Corinthians 2:11). His mind gives us access to hidden treasures stored in secret places (Isaiah 45:3).

One of my goals in writing this book is to lead you to engage more deeply with the mind of Christ by the power of the Holy Spirit. This opens the portal to an infinitely deep well of divine imagination, ingenuity, inspiration, and innovation. Your mind is limited in its ability to imagine, visualize, conceptualize, etc. Yet the mind of Christ is unlimited, which means the possibilities of what could be accomplished by Him through you are endless.

One of the amazing things about the mind of Christ is that it allows you to see the invisible things that God's grace has already completed on your behalf. Therefore, you don't need to spend unnecessary time trying to conjure up something when all you have to do is see what God has already produced and agree with what He has done in order to bring it into manifestation.

⟨⟨⟨❖⟩⟩⟩

B.I.G. Idea:
A mind constantly washed in the Word becomes
fertile ground for God ideas.

⟨⟨⟨❖⟩⟩⟩

Your success in business has already been established based on what God has ordained for you. Now you must see it so that you can possess it. This is why it's so necessary for you to embrace and engage the mind of Christ. A union between your mind and His will elevate your planning process into a time of revealing and unveiling what God wants you to do versus you trying to develop something "good" out of your own thoughts. This leads us to V-STAR…

Getting Started With V-STAR

Strategic planning is a spiritual activity when the Holy Spirit directs it. God even declared that He has plans for us, which are good and prosperous (Jeremiah 29:11). Our job as Kingdom building entrepreneurs is to incorporate His plans into our businesses. This strategic planning model will help you to do just that.

V-STAR – which stands for Vision, Strategy, Target, Action, and Results – is a God-inspired strategic planning tool. In addition to divine revelation, in creating this system, I was able to draw on more than a decade of experience as a respected consultant to corporations, small businesses, non-profits, and professionals at all levels. This is a simple and focused process to help you build structure around your business idea. It is simple because it asks the six basic questions of your business idea, which are *Why, What, Who, When, Where, and How?* It is also a great tool that you can revisit and use for on-going strategic planning.

This system can not only be applied for the overall strategic planning process of your company, but you can utilize it to develop strategies within the different functional areas of your business, including operations, product development, marketing and sales, human resources, customer service, financial planning, and more. This literally can become the planning and management DNA within your company that allows you to cultivate a culture that seeks God for spiritual direction and practical execution.

Triple Bottom Line

One of the key things about developing your vision is your perspective on money and how you will ultimately measure your success. Some Christian entrepreneurs still wrestle with the fact that it is OK with God if you are prosperous. Therefore, they often try to downplay the financial aspects of their business. The truth is if you don't have a profitable business that is sustainable, you will eventually go out of business.

If you have a problem with money, you shouldn't go into business. God doesn't have a problem with you making a lot of money in your business. However, He does have a problem with you idolizing money. That is why I believe it is important for Kingdom CEOs to have a more holistic perspective of success to keep the money issue within the right frame of reference. I call this the "Triple Bottom Line."

I did not invent this term, but the overall concept is very relevant to this discussion. If you research it you will find that social entrepreneurs and those focused in the corporate social responsibility arena use it in reference to businesses measuring their impact on people and the planet in addition to their financial results.

While I believe these criteria are a good, broad-based way to measure the overall impact of a business, I am proposing a somewhat different set of measurement standards for Kingdom entrepreneurs. I believe you should measure the holistic success of your business in these three ways:

1) **Financial:** Monetary profits. This is the easiest, tangible measure of the three.

2) **Spiritual:** The impact you have for the Kingdom of God. You have to reconcile this with what you believe He called you to do with your business.

3) **Social:** The influence you have on the people God called you to reach directly or indirectly through your business. This includes customers, employees, suppliers, partners, and the broader community in which you operate.

Triple Bottom Line

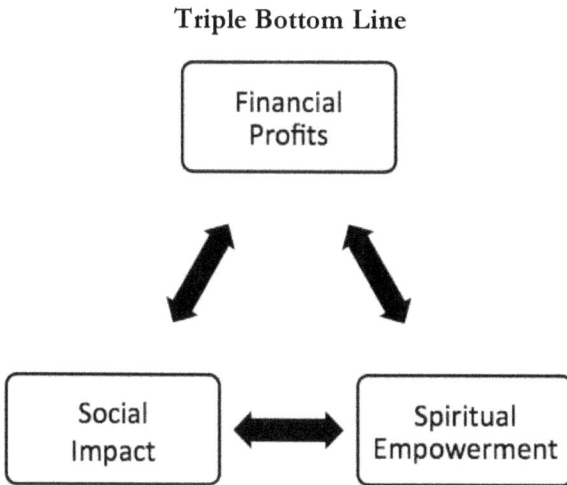

When your vision and operating activities incorporate all three of these aspects, you will not be consumed by the thought of money and will have a healthy approach in your decision-making. As I stated in the introduction of this book, this operational philosophy closely resembles the global evangelism strategy of Business as Mission (BAM), or as I call it, Business as Ministry. BAM takes the world's embrace of social entrepreneurship and adds the spiritual component of intentionally incorporating Kingdom principles in your business operations. Transformed lives is what God ultimately is in pursuit of through your enterprise, so BAM is an excellent platform to connect spiritual outreach and engagement with normal day to day activities. I will continue to unfold layers of this strategy in the coming chapters.

Developing Your Vision Statement

It is the greatest honor to be asked by God to do something big for Him. Unfortunately, many Christian leaders here the initial idea from God, but don't stick around long enough to get all the instructions on how to build the business, ministry, community organization, etc. The bigger the idea the more details He will need to give you to ensure that it is successful and sustainable. God gave Moses very specific and detailed instructions on how He wanted every aspect of the tabernacle built, including the furniture inside and the clothes that the priests would wear. He didn't leave any room for guessing or for Moses' own interpretation. Unfortunately, many of us spend a lot of time dealing with trial and error in our businesses, because we didn't take the time to get all the instructions from God. Don't try to build God's vision with your ideas or in your own strength.

In the V-STAR System, the Vision component includes your Mission and Values. Your business vision statement defines and clarifies success for what you see in the future for you, your company, your target market and related stakeholders if your business achieves its stated goals and objectives. Here are some characteristics of well-written vision statements:

⇨ Describes your company's ultimate "big picture."
⇨ Aligns with your values.
⇨ Inspired by your passions.
⇨ Can't be accomplished by you alone (if it can be then it's too small).
⇨ Short-term and long-term perspective.
⇨ Extends beyond your lifetime.

A few questions to get you started:
⇨ What is your dream?
⇨ If money were no object, what would you do if it were guaranteed that you couldn't fail?
⇨ Who will benefit from your vision?
⇨ Where do you see your company 3 years from now? 10 years? 20 years?

My Vision Statement

Here are some questions to ask yourself after you have written your first draft:

⇨ Is it too broad that it's vague and undefined?
⇨ Is it so narrow there's no growth opportunities?
⇨ Is it exclusive or inclusive?
⇨ Is it innovative versus strange?
⇨ Does it inspire others to want to get involved?
⇨ Does it paint a picture that you/others will know when it's actually happening?

*Note: If you need additional help, search the Internet for some examples.

Developing Your Business Mission Statement

Your business mission statement defines and clarifies why you are in business and what you will do to achieve your vision. Here are some characteristics of well-written mission statements:

⇨ Describes "why" your company exists.
⇨ Aligns with your values.
⇨ Flows out of your life's mission.
⇨ Provides daily direction, realignment, and inspiration.
⇨ Clear and easy to understand.
⇨ Action oriented.
⇨ No clichés.

A few questions to get you started:

⇨ What do you want your company to be known for?
⇨ What type of legacy do you want to build?
⇨ How do you want to impact people, communities, or organizations?
⇨ What is your company passionate about doing?

PAUL WILSON, JR.

My Mission Statement

Here are some questions to ask yourself after you have written your first draft:

⇨ Does it give your company a sense of purpose and direction?
⇨ Does it inspire you and others?
⇨ Is it bold or aggressive?
⇨ Is it flexible, i.e. the mission doesn't have to change just because the business model does?
⇨ Is it too "text book" or it duplicates someone else's?
⇨ Can you use it as a company slogan?

*Note: If you need some additional help, search the Internet for some examples.

Developing Your Values Statement

Your business values statement defines and clarifies how you will operate your business. Here are some characteristics of solid values statements:

⇨ Communicate your company's character.

⇨ Inspired by your personal values/convictions.

⇨ Clear and easy to understand.

⇨ Behavioral boundaries for owner, employees, partnerships, etc.

⇨ How you will interact in your relationships.

What will be C.O.R.E. to your business success?:

⇨ Culture

⇨ Outlook

⇨ Relationships

⇨ Energy

A few questions to get you started:

⇨ What C.O.R.E. principles will guide your decision-making?

⇨ How will you do business?

⇨ What do I want my company to become known for?

*Note: If you need some additional help, search the Internet for some examples.

My Values Statement

Cultivating Your Company Culture

God never intended for the Ten Commandments to be read and not lived. Likewise, in any organization it is not enough to just have important documents written in operations or employee manuals, such as your vision, mission, values, goals, etc. These would be considered "logos" words. You have to build your culture around by integrating each of these components into all aspects of your organization so that they come alive, which would be considered "rhema" words.

You must determine how to creatively incorporate what's written into on-going activities, such as meetings, marketing campaigns, signage, contests, employee evaluations, recruiting, incentives, customer service, and social media, among other considerations. All of these individual activities collectively help you to reinforce the organization's core values and beliefs into each person in the organization.

The topic of company culture is extremely important, because it determines the type of atmosphere that you will have to create and cultivate to ultimately accomplish your God-given vision. Your company culture is comprised of your vision, mission, values, beliefs, behaviors, symbols, policies, language, customs, norms, and any other formal and informal characteristics that reflect the true nature and aspirations of who you are as an organization. The development of your company culture should be intentional, but it is also something that grows organically over time.

Within the Body of Christ our goal should be to duplicate the culture that is demonstrated in Heaven (Matthew 6:10). Scripture gives us indicators of how to do this on a personal level. In Galatians 5:22-23, Apostle Paul lists the "Fruit of the Spirit," which are character traits that should be evident in every Christian. These character traits should influence every environment in which we operate. I call these "spiritual best practices."

As a Kingdom CEO, shaping your company culture involves translating these spiritual best practices into business best practices. It just makes sense for us to utilize the Bible to help shape our business ideas and activities. The Fruit of the Spirit should also be evident as "fruit" in your business. Another way to think about this is that you are replicating the culture of the Kingdom of Heaven – God's will, wisdom, ways, and works – into the marketplace.

Look at the following table to see practical examples of how you can apply the Fruit of Spirit in your business. In the last column you can write specific activities that you can implement in your business.

Spiritual Fruit Translated to Business Best Practices

Spiritual Best Practices	Business Best Practices	Practical Application
Love	Focus on serving customers and meeting needs, not making money (as a priority) Genuinely caring for customer and employees needs Selflessness displayed consistently	
Joy	Passion Excitement Contagious attitude	
Peace	Mediators of conflict Settle conflicts quickly and fairly Cooperative relationships Win-win partnerships	
Kindness	Fanatical commitment to customer service Environment to fail safely Exceed expectations Generosity	
Goodness	Proactively providing solutions that help people Business excellence Creativity and innovation Industry leader	
Faithfulness	Stay true to your brand Integrity in all dealings Moral and ethical practices Consistency of purpose	
Meekness	Servant leadership Power/influence under control Strength of character "Humbition": Humble yet boldly ambitions	
Self-Control	Visionary: Always act with the end in mind Disciplined thought, action, words Streamlined, efficient operations	

《《《❖》》》

B.I.G. Idea:
The Bible is the best source for business best practices!

《《《❖》》》

CHAPTER 7

STRATEGIZING MY SUCCESS

"Of Issachar, men who had understanding of the times, to know what
Israel ought to do..."
1 Chronicles 12:32

V-STAR BUSINESS PLANNING SYSTEM

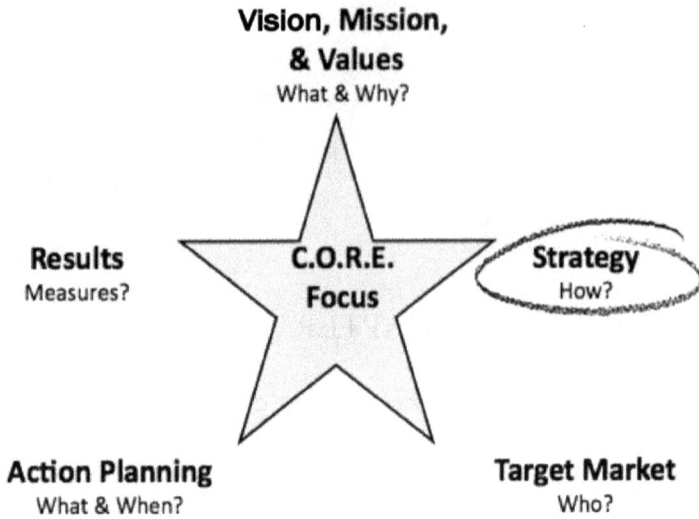

**Vision, Mission,
& Values**
What & Why?

Results
Measures?

**C.O.R.E.
Focus**

Strategy
How?

Action Planning
What & When?

Target Market
Who?

Strategizing Your Success

When you are on an unfamiliar path in business it can be very hard to cut through the clutter of advice and best practices from everybody who thinks they have the best way forward. Your number priority as a Kingdom CEO is to hear the voice of the Lord and following His instructions. His leadership may take you places that you never expected to go or where it seems nobody is moving. However, He sees the end from the beginning, so it is essential to follow Him without question. Your obedience could be the difference between life and death for your business, the timing between a securing major contract and missing the meeting, or being in the right place at the right time to meet the right person who was waiting for the right opportunity to invest in. Learning how to trust God and follow His Spirit in business is critical to your success.

God never does anything haphazardly or without a strategy. Everything He does is thoroughly planned and executed, decently and in order. The best example of this was His plan to redeem mankind back to Himself. He designed a strategy with Jesus at the center of it, and with you and I as the primary beneficiaries. He providentially incorporated all the critical and necessary elements, so that everything would happen at the right time in the right place with the right people.

A strategy is the process by which you identify, evaluate, engage, and solve problems that lead to your success. Your success will not be coincidental, incidental, or accidental. Your success will only happen when you are strategic and intentional about doing the right things at the right time with the right people.

The success of your Kingdom business is not going to happen just because you have a good idea or you prayed for success to happen. You must have well-defined strategy that is executed on a daily basis. A strategy is what drives your business forward with clarity and cohesiveness. Without it you will have lots of activities, but no real results to show for them. You may be busy, but not necessarily productive.

《《❖》》

B.I.G. Idea:
Your success will not be incidental, coincidental, or accidental.
Your success will be intentional.

《《❖》》

Strategic Revelation

As a Kingdom building entrepreneur, one of the things you have to be very careful of is that you don't start relying on your knowledge or experience without consulting the Holy Spirit. The temptation you must fight against is to lean unto your own understanding instead of acknowledging God in all of your ways and allowing Him to direct your paths. Although you are very intelligent and talented, you still have major limitations and weaknesses that only God's grace and wisdom can enable you to overcome.

A great example of someone relying on God for a strategic plan is King David in 2 Samuel 5:17-25.

"When the Philistines heard that David had been anointed king over Israel, all the Philistines went up to search for David. But David heard of it and went down to the stronghold. Now the Philistines had come and spread out in the Valley of Rephaim. And David inquired of the LORD, "Shall I go up against the Philistines? Will you give them into my hand?" And the LORD said to David, "Go up, for I will certainly give the Philistines into your hand." And David came to Baal-perazim, and David defeated them there. And he said, "The LORD has broken through my enemies before me like a breaking flood." Therefore the name of that place is called Baal-perazim. And the Philistines left their idols there, and David and his men carried them away. And the Philistines came up yet again and spread out in the Valley of Rephaim. And when David inquired of the LORD, he said, "You shall not go up; go around to their rear, and come against them opposite the balsam trees. And when you hear the sound of marching in the tops of the balsam trees, then rouse yourself, for then the LORD has gone out before you to strike down the army of the Philistines." And David did as the LORD commanded him, and struck down the Philistines from Geba to Gezer."

As you can see in the first part of this passage, David asked God if he could utilize a strategy of directly pursuing and attacking the Philistines, and God's affirmative answer assured him of victory. However, later in the passage when it came time for David to fight against the Philistines again, he inquired of the Lord and received a different strategy he was to utilize to defeat the Philistines. David was wise enough to know that he needed to employ God's strategy in order to defeat his enemy. If he had only relied on his knowledge, talent, or experience acquired in previous clashes, he probably would have lost these battles.

Don't fall into the trap of relying on your own wits or qualifications and leaving God out of your strategic planning process. Be like Apostle Paul as it relates to comparing your resume to the surpassing worth of knowing and gaining Christ (Philippians 3:8). The truth is what you bring to the table is miniscule in comparison to what God has planned to give you, which includes strategies for success.

* * * * *

"Call to me and I will answer you, and will tell you great and hidden things
that you have not known."
Jeremiah 33:3

* * * * *

Give the Holy Spirit permission to be your closest advisor. If you stay connected with God, He will give you the strategies needed to conquer your competitors in the marketplace.

Establishing Your Goals

We are first going to focus on developing your goals and then use those to create your strategy for success. For a strategy to be most effective, it must centered on goals that are relevant, well defined, and attainable.

Goals allow you to break down your vision and mission into bite-size chunks that you can use as checkpoints to know how well you are progressing. Business goals are quantitative and qualitative milestones or benchmarks that measure the progress of your vision, mission, and business performance. Goals are like your business "bulls-eye," which provide you with a clear target of the direction in which your business is going and the pace at which it is getting there.

Here are some characteristics of well-written goals:
- ✓ Quantifies your vision and mission statements.
- ✓ Gives you a target to shoot for.
- ✓ Provides substance and direction for performance management.
- ✓ Scorecard to track performance and progress (i.e., financial, operational, customers, sales, facilities, customer service).
- ✓ SMART: Specific, Measurable, Attainable, Realistic and Timely?

A few questions to get you started:
- ⇨ What are your short-term and long-term goals (monthly, quarterly, annually)?
- ⇨ In terms of the Triple Bottom Line, what are my financial, spiritual, and social goals? How do I quantify my progress in these areas?
- ⇨ What do you see your company accomplishing 5 years from now? 10 years? 20 years?
- ⇨ How much do you desire the company to be worth (financial value)?
- ⇨ What are your conservative in-the-box goals versus stretch-your-faith out-the-box goals?

PAUL WILSON, JR.

My Goals

Here are some questions to ask yourself after you have written your first draft:

⇨ Are you afraid to dream big?

⇨ Was I too conservative (in-the-box) vs. stretching my thinking (out-the-box)?

⇨ Do your goals align with industry standards?

⇨ How is technology going to impact your business model?

⇨ Do you expect your business model to change over the next 3 to 5 years?

*Note: If you need some additional help, search the Internet for examples of goals related to your business or industry.

Strategy Building Blocks

A business strategy is used to implement plans and execute ideas in order to effectively and efficiently accomplish your goals. In order for a strategy that you develop to be relevant and reliable, a thorough analysis of your company's current condition must be conducted. Even if you have not started your business yet, this is a very important exercise to undertake.

Your strategy does not exist in a vacuum or separate from the operations of your company. No matter how large or small, simple or complicated, every businesses performs certain critical activities that can be separated into these five core functions:

1) **People**: Your comprehensive human resource capacity and capabilities.
2) **Products & Services**: The products and/or services that you sell to generate revenues. This area also includes the marketing of those goods and services.
3) **Processes**: Step by step activities used to deliver and support your business operations.
4) **Performance Management**: Criteria used to monitor, measure, and make adjustments to your current operations for the purpose of continuous improvement and growth.
5) **Profit Management**: Goals, measures, and activities used to manage and grow the financial performance of the business.

SWOT Analysis

SWOT - which stands for Strengths, Weaknesses, Opportunities, and Threats - is a tool to get an accurate assessment of your company's current condition and competitive environment. A thorough SWOT should be the foundation and focus of your company's strategy.

SWOT Matrix

	Positive	Challenges
Internal	**STRENGTHS**	**WEAKNESSES**
External	**OPPORTUNITIES**	**THREATS**

Internal Strengths
✓ Resources and capabilities that can be used as a basis for developing a competitive advantage.
✓ Consider areas such as human resources, special skills, financial resources, unique product/service, technology, internal processes, etc.
✓ Be confident in what you are good at.

Internal Weaknesses
✓ Areas where the company needs to make improvements.
✓ Other areas where an overused strength might have a negative impact on the company.
✓ Sell your strengths and buy your weaknesses. In other words focus on what you do best and look for partnership where you are weak.

External Opportunities
✓ New marketplace opportunities for profit and growth.
✓ Opportunities to capitalize on customer trends or competitors' problems.
✓ Grow or die! Anything healthy should be growing. Be willing to step outside of your comfort zone to take advantage of the *right* opportunities.

External Threats
✓ Changes in the external environment that may have a negative impact on your company, such as customer trends, competitors' activities, or the overall economic environment.
✓ Trends that could have future ramifications even if they are not problems for you today.
✓ Know the strengths and weaknesses of your competitors.

Strategy Development Process:
1) Perform a SWOT Analysis by evaluating your business's core functions through the filter of the four SWOT areas (see SWOT Matrix with Core Functions on the next page).
2) Rate all the items you listed in your SWOT analysis in terms of priority or potential impact (3-high, 2-medium, 1-low).
3) Review each list and identify 5 overall critical strategic issues or themes based on the ratings. Focus on the "high" and "medium" rated issues.
4) Brainstorm ideas that could address the key strategic issues you identified for your company.

5) Develop specific action plans to address your company's key strategic issues.
6) Use the core functions to structure and link your plans in a strategy map.

SWOT Matrix with Core Functions

Internal Strengths	Internal Weaknesses
1.People 2.Products & Services 3.Processes 4.Performance Management 5.Profit Management	1.People 2.Products & Services 3.Processes 4.Performance Management 5.Profit Management
External Opportunities	External Threats
1.People 2.Products & Services 3.Processes 4.Performance Management 5.Profit Management	1.People 2.Products & Services 3.Processes 4.Performance Management 5.Profit Management

Business Structure

The right business structure plays a major role in the execution of your strategy. Having the appropriate legal business structure will position you to be responsible to run your business "properly and in order" (1 Corinthians 14:10), "know the state of your flocks" (Proverbs 27:23), and "render unto Caesar what is Caesar's" (Mark 12:17).

There are several options for legal business structures that you are available to you including (Source: Small Business Administration, www.sba.gov):

1) **Sole Proprietorship**: A sole proprietorship is the most basic type of business to establish. You alone own the company and are responsible for its assets and liabilities. Learn more about the sole proprietor structure.
2) **Corporation**: A corporation is more complex and generally suggested for larger, established companies with multiple employees. Learn more about how Corporations are structured.
3) **Limited Liability Company (LLC)**: An LLC is designed to provide the limited liability features of a corporation and the tax efficiencies and operational flexibility of a partnership. Learn more about how LLCs are structured.

4) **Cooperative**: People form cooperatives to meet a collective need or to provide a service that benefits all member-owners. Learn more about how cooperatives are structured.

5) **Partnership**: An LLC is designed to provide the limited liability features of a corporation and the tax efficiencies and operational flexibility of a partnership. Learn more about how LLCs are structured.

6) **S Corporation**: An S corporation is similar to a C corporation but you are taxed only on the personal level. Learn more about how S corporations are structured.

7) **B-Corporation:** A class of corporation required by law to create general benefit for society as well as for shareholders. Benefit corporations must create a material positive impact on society, and consider how their decisions affect their employees, community, and the environment. Moreover, they must publicly report on their social and environmental performances using established third-party standards. Laws have been passed in 12 states so far creating this new business structure. Go to www.bcorporation.net to learn if you are in one of those states and if your type of business would fall under this type of structure.

This is just a high level summary of different legal structures. Prior to choosing any of these, I highly recommend you consult with a business attorney and a Certified Public Accountant (CPA). They will help you to choose the right legal structure and order your finances so that you can be a good steward over your business and stay out of trouble with Uncle Sam. You also need to connect with your state and local governments to inquire about the correct licenses that are applicable to your business.

Corporate and Government Supplier Diversity Certifications

As you are evaluating your ideal target customer, depending the ownership structure of your business, you might be able to take advantage of corporate and/or governmental supplier diversity programs. Supplier Diversity is a business contracting initiative that proactively promotes the use of minority owned, women owned, veteran owned, historically underutilized geographic regions, and SBA defined small business vendors as suppliers.

Corporations as well as local, state, and federal government agencies have different flavors of these programs. These may be viable customers for your product or service. If you are interested in pursuing supplier diversity opportunities with corporations or governments make sure you do your homework so you can find the right fits for your business. You can also contact me directly. I have a lot of previous career and consulting experience working with these programs.

Creating a Strategy Map

A strategy map is a tool used to visually represent specific objectives, initiatives, and actions needed to accomplish a company's overall strategy. Key benefits of using a strategy map include having the ability to:

1) Directly address high priority issues identified in your SWOT analysis.
2) Identify strategic needs that reach across multiple functions of the company.
3) Focus on opportunities to increase efficiency and improve productivity.
4) Pinpoint problem areas in the execution of your strategic plan.
5) Create specific daily/weekly action items that link directly to high-level goals.

Strategy Map Components:

⇨ **Goals**: Quantitative or qualitative milestones or benchmarks that measure the progress of your vision, mission, and business performance.

⇨ **Objectives**: High level, measurable targets that will result in accomplishing your company's goals.

⇨ **Initiatives**: Specific steps required to accomplish the objectives.

⇨ **Actions Items**: Specific activities used to accomplish the strategic initiatives.

Strategy Map Instructions: A separate strategy map should be developed for each of your company's goals and/or core functions.

1) Write your company's overall goals (use your quarterly or annual goals). Focus on quantitative measures in the five core functions; but based on your current situation or business model, you might not incorporate all five.

2) Write two to three specific, high level objectives needed to accomplish each goal. Focus on quantitative measures.

3) For each objective write two to three specific initiatives to accomplish those objectives.

4) For each initiative write as many action items as needed to accomplish each initiative.

5) Be sure that you incorporate problem areas you identified in your SWOT analysis and solutions brainstorming.

6) Once you are satisfied with your final version, use flip charts that you can post onto a wall in your work area and leave them there so that you have a constant reminder of where you are in your implementation process and timeline.

Sample Strategy Map

Goals	Objectives	Initiatives	Actions

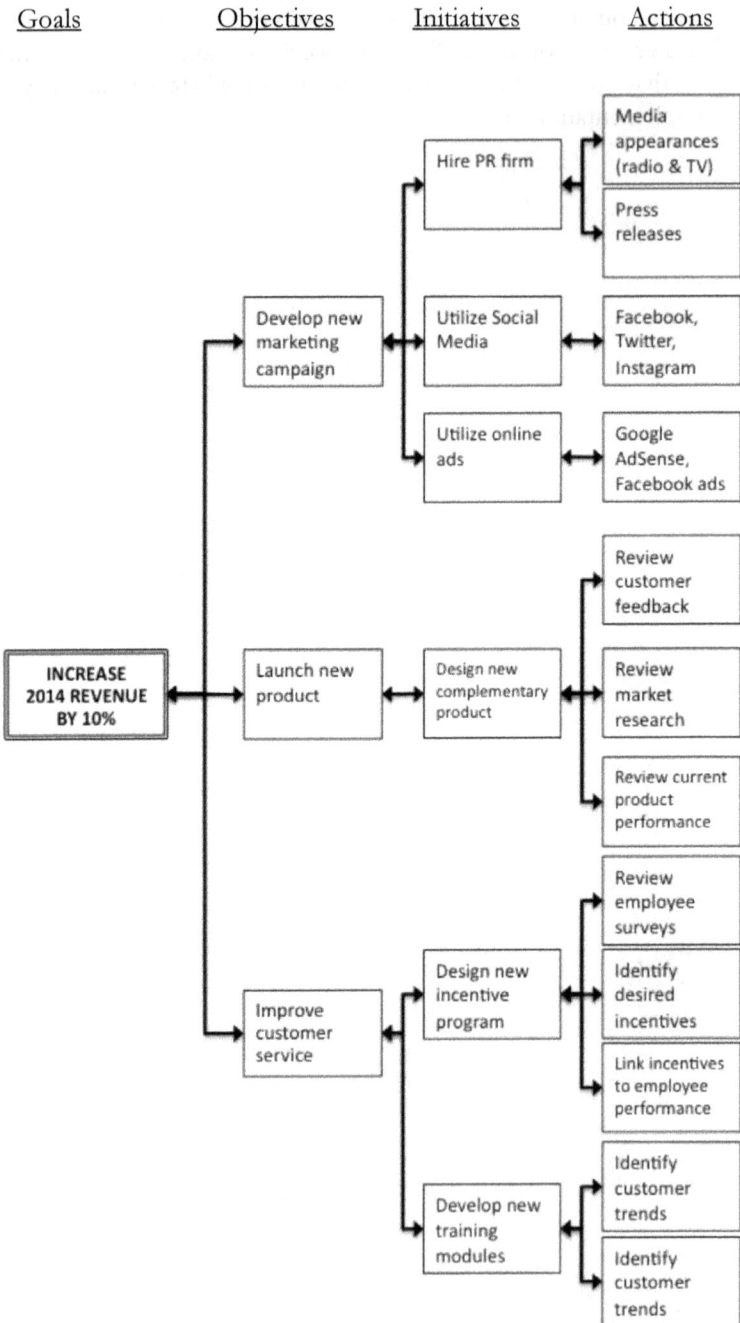

			Media appearances (radio & TV)
		Hire PR firm	Press releases
	Develop new marketing campaign	Utilize Social Media	Facebook, Twitter, Instagram
		Utilize online ads	Google AdSense, Facebook ads
			Review customer feedback
INCREASE 2014 REVENUE BY 10%	Launch new product	Design new complementary product	Review market research
			Review current product performance
			Review employee surveys
	Improve customer service	Design new incentive program	Identify desired incentives
			Link incentives to employee performance
			Identify customer trends
		Develop new training modules	Identify customer trends

Sample Strategy Map

Goals   Objectives   Initiatives   Actions

CHAPTER 8

BUILDING MY DREAM TEAM

"He makes the whole body fit together perfectly. As each part does its own special work, it helps the other parts grow, so that the whole body is healthy and growing and full of love."
Ephesians 4:16

V-STAR BUSINESS PLANNING SYSTEM

**Vision, Mission,
& Values**
What & Why?

Results
Measures?

**C.O.R.E.
Focus**

Strategy
How?

Action Planning
What & When?

Target Market
Who?

Partnership is God's Idea

God never intended for us operate in isolation in anything connected to what He wants to accomplish. In Genesis 1:26 we can see how He set the standard for partnership when the Trinity collaborated to create us in His image. The power of partnership that they modeled in Heaven is now supposed to be replicated by us on earth.

Throughout Scripture God ordained and blessed divinely inspired joint ventures. Some examples include Christ and the church, husbands and wives, David and Jonathan, and Jesus and his Disciples. In Matthew 18:20 Jesus declares that he will be in the midst when two or three come to gather in his name. Ephesians 4:16 and Romans 12:4-8 speak to the spiritual advantages of Christians combining their individual talents, gifting, anointing, and resources with other Christians.

Our spiritual assets have a somewhat limited capacity when used independently or in isolation. However, an exponential power is activated when we link up with other Believers. Something special happens when Christians intentionally and strategically connect with others who have complementary spiritual gifts and talents. One can put to flight one thousand, but two can put to flight ten thousand (Deuteronomy 32:30).

Apostle Paul is probably one of the best examples we can look at the see the practice and profits of partnership. We rarely if ever hear of Paul going anywhere or doing anything by himself. He valued relationships for their spiritual and practical value. He writes in 2 Corinthians 8:23, *"If anyone asks about Titus, say that he is my partner who works with me to help you. And these brothers are representatives of the churches. They are splendid examples of those who bring glory to Christ."*

〈〈〈❖〉〉〉

B.I.G. Idea:

Find out whom God called you to work with. An exponential power is activated when you link your spiritual assets together with other Believers.

〈〈〈❖〉〉〉

The First Organizational Management Consultant

Structure and organization are spiritual principles with very practical implications. In Exodus 18, Jethro's advice to Moses saved him from a lot of stress and may have added some years to his life. We also see organizational leadership strategies used in the New Testament church (Acts 6:1-7), which benefited the Apostles and those in the community. Let's look at three principles of divinely inspired organizational management:

1) **Delegated authority**: If God understands the benefit of delegating His power and authority, why shouldn't you? Follow the leader. Delegation also allows the leader of the organization to think more strategically versus getting bogged down needlessly in day-to-day details.

2) **Division of labor:** Teamwork expands your company's capabilities. Breaking down big projects into smaller jobs creates the opportunity for people to work in the land of their giftedness. This is also a great way to discover new leaders in your organization.

3) **Dynamic celebrations:** When the right people are in the right positions doing the right jobs they are more likely to get great results and accomplish your goals. This builds sense of shared value and ownership in the project or organization that is infectious and momentous.

Teamwork Makes the Kingdom Work

The twelfth chapter of Romans paints an incredible picture of how the Body of Christ is made up of many different, unique, and gifted members who operate interdependently. Ephesians 4:16 builds on that by making reference to the fact that when every gift is operating in its specialty, the Body of Christ can operate at full capacity and every need in the family of God is met. When every Christian is in place and doing what God called them to do, the results are beneficial corporately and individually.

I have heard this principle taught many times, especially at local churches in relation to getting everyone in congregations involved in serving in ministries. However, I have rarely if ever heard it taught that Christians in business should operate in the same manner in the marketplace and can reap similar benefits, organizationally and personally. Whether we are talking about inside an individual business or multiple businesses partnering together, exponential potential is ignited when the separate parts sync together and work in harmony.

$$\langle\langle\langle\diamond\rangle\rangle\rangle$$

B.I.G. Idea:

The greatest accomplishments you will have your life and business will happen through collaboration.

$$\langle\langle\langle\diamond\rangle\rangle\rangle$$

We see a great example of the exponential profit potential that is available for Kingdom business partnerships in Luke 5:7. In this account a group of fisherman literally would have lost their incredible blessing and their boat if they had not partnered with another boat to haul in the massive harvest of fish that Jesus blessed them with. I am sure he already knew how big the blessing was going to be. So part of the lesson for the disciples was to see how they would handle abundant increase.

Unfortunately, too many Christian entrepreneurs have a "lone ranger" mentality and are struggling because they are trying to go it alone. They have not understood the power and potential of partnership. They are unaware that God provides an anointed synergy and profitability for those who work together in unity toward His purposes. Kingdom CEOs would do themselves well to listen to the wisdom of Solomon on this matter:

> *"Two are better than one, because they have a good reward for their toil. 10For if they fall, one will lift up his fellow. But woe to him who is alone when he falls and has not another to lift him up!... And though a man might prevail against one who is alone, two will withstand him — a threefold cord is not quickly [easily] broken."* Ecclesiastes 4:9-12

You are certainly gifted and empowered by God to do great exploits. Nevertheless, the most significant things that happen in the Kingdom are the result of partnerships with multiple Believers. The reason is that isolation breeds independence, but partnership builds interdependence that increases your capacity for exponential success.

〈〈〈❖〉〉〉

B.I.G. Idea:
Isolation breeds independence, but partnership builds interdependence, which increases your capacity for exponential success.

〈〈〈❖〉〉〉

Benefits of a Dream Team

People are the most important assets of any business. Therefore, building a strong team around you must become a priority so that your business will have the best chance of long-term success. No matter how good your products, services, technology, etc., any business that does not value and enhance the development of it's human resources will eventually crumble from the inside out.

The reality for most entrepreneurs is that they are not going to start off with a fully staffed organization. Still, you must recruit and engage partners who support your vision, share your values, specialize in the areas that are not your strengths, and present mutually beneficial opportunities to grow. I call this your Dream Team.

When you have this strong team of people connected to your business,

they perform several important roles, including:
- ⇨ **Counsel:** Provide alternative perspectives for your decision-making. Help you identify and maneuver around hazards. Assist in shaping and executing the vision.
- ⇨ **Connections:** Expand your access to relationships outside of your current circle.
- ⇨ **Capacity:** Increase your ability to handle more business. Complementary skills and experience expand your expertise for customer solutions.
- ⇨ **Creativity:** Develop new ideas and pursue opportunities with outside the box collaborative thinking.
- ⇨ **Correction:** Help you fix what's broken in your business. Provide discipline for operations that lack structure.
- ⇨ **Capital:** Access to financial resources outside of your current access.
- ⇨ **Confidence:** Nurture support and encouragement during difficult periods.

Your Dream Team could take several different forms, but I will highlight three here:
1. **Board of Directors:** A formal relationship with a group of individuals that are bound with fiduciary responsibility to the company based on the by-laws.
2. **Vision Council:** An informal group of advisors with no fiduciary or legal responsibility to your company. This structure is great for helping you be accountable with your vision to a group of leaders that you trust, but without pressure on them of legal responsibility on your council members.
3. **Professional Partnerships:** Strategic relationships with other businesses or leaders for the purpose of pursuing and fulfilling business opportunities jointly.

It is very possible that these professional partners could eventually become part of your organization permanently. However, prior to that time you must be on the same page with each one individually as to whether you will have a formal or informal working relationship. It is best that you put your relationship in writing with a Memorandum of Understanding (MOU) so that both parties know exactly what is expected of each other, especially as it relates to financial matters. This document does not have to be long or complicated, but it must be clear about each partner's role so as to avoid unnecessary conflicts.

* * * * *

"Great vision without great people is irrelevant."
~ Jim Collins

* * * * *

Structuring Your Dream Team

A necessary element of planning your Dream Team is structuring your organization the right way with the right people in the right positions. Even if you start off as a solo entrepreneur, it is important that you begin visualizing the desired structure and size of your future organization. This will encourage you to start planning today that which will lead you to where you eventually want to be in the future.

Here are five steps you need to take to move forward with structuring your Dream Team:

1) Create an organizational chart based on the size and structure for the type of business you are forming.
   - ✓ Visualize the future.
   - ✓ Create the ideal structure (review successful companies in your industry to see how their structured).
   - ✓ Write job descriptions for each position.
   - ✓ Prioritize key positions in terms of your company's strategic needs.
   - ✓ Maintain flexibility.

2) Develop team member job success profiles based on essential knowledge, skills, and behaviors (culture) needed to operate the business (see sample at end of chapter).
   - ✓ Knowledge: What they need to know how to do.
   - ✓ Skills: What they need to be able to do (incorporate T.A.G.S.).
   - ✓ Behavior: How they should work (reference your values statement).

3) Recruit your Dream Team using your vision, mission, and values as filters.
   - ✓ Partners: Strategic leaders who provide specific resources to the business (management, operations, services, etc.). They could be inside or outside of the business.
   - ✓ Employees: Full-time and part-time paid team members individuals who have specific responsibilities.

- ✓ Interns: Unpaid team members, typically students, who have specific responsibilities.
- ✓ Advisors: Key individuals external to the business who provide strategic advice, but are not responsible for daily operations.

4) Delegate responsibilities.
- ✓ Clear definitions.
- ✓ Be flexible.
- ✓ Allow for empowered decision making.
- ✓ Embrace accountability.

5) Manage performance expectations and objectives.
- ✓ You can't "expect" what you don't "inspect."
- ✓ Objectivity vs. subjectivity (performance over personality)
- ✓ Link individual metrics to company performance objectives/metrics.
- ✓ Create incentive programs to engage and energize all the players on the team.

Whatever God ordains He will sustain. That includes the human talent that's needed to increase the capacity of your organization so that you can service more people or handle more customers. He never meant for you to have to do anything by yourself and for yourself for entire existence of your enterprise. Furthermore, if you stay diligent to your call, He will not just sent bodies, He will send skilled laborers who excel in their craft. God has prepared His best for you, including the human resources that will help grow your organization.

Sample Organizational Chart

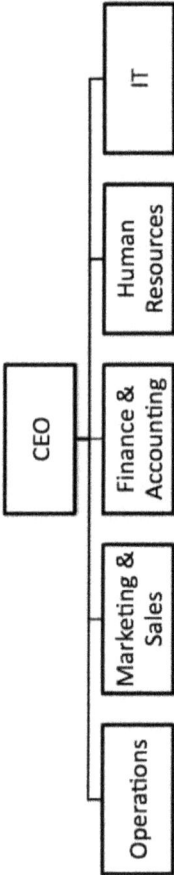

```
                    ┌─────────┐
                    │   CEO   │
                    └────┬────┘
        ┌────────────┬───┴────────────┬────────────┐
  ┌───────────┐ ┌───────────┐ ┌───────────┐ ┌───────────┐ ┌──────┐
  │Operations │ │Marketing &│ │Finance &  │ │  Human    │ │  IT  │
  │           │ │  Sales    │ │Accounting │ │ Resources │ │      │
  └───────────┘ └───────────┘ └───────────┘ └───────────┘ └──────┘
```

Sample Job Success Profile

Position Title: _____

Reports To: _____

Roles & Responsibilities: You will be responsible for fulfilling the following requirements...
   1)
   2)
   3)
   4)
   5)

Skills: You must have a superior ability, competence, and talent to perform the following...
   1)
   2)
   3)
   4)
   5)

Character/Behavior: The principles and values that shape our company culture in pursuit of our company mission. Each team member agrees to uphold and promote these values in our daily work.
   1)
   2)
   3)
   4)
   5)

Exercise: Create your Dream Team Strategy Map

CHAPTER 9

TARGETING MY IDEAL CUSTOMER

"… and you will be my witnesses in Jerusalem, and in all Judea and Samaria, and to the ends of the earth."
Acts 1:8

V-STAR BUSINESS PLANNING SYSTEM

**Vision, Mission,
& Values**
What & Why?

Results
Measures?

**C.O.R.E.
Focus**

Strategy
How?

Action Planning
What & When?

Target Market
Who?

Kingdom Positioning

In the Old Testament God placed a lot of emphasis on geographic locations, especially in relation to the promise land for the children of Israel. Connected to those places usually included references to His presence, provision, prosperity, protection, peace, and power.

Many Christians reference the story of Jabez when they discus the concept of God increasing their territory and influence (1 Chronicles 4:9-11). What I don't hear most of them talk about is the fact that when he prayed for God to expand his territory, it wasn't just a spiritual request. Jabez was most likely referencing a specific geographic region, because he possessed a city (1 Chronicles 2:55).

Likewise, there is a place of prosperity that God has already assigned to you. It's connected to a certain group of people or an industry He has called you to operate and succeed in. Obedience opens doors to the places of prosperity, but disobedience closes them. If you don't follow His plans for you, you will be out of the place God has already created for you to prosper.

God told Jeremiah that he was called for a specific purpose before he was born (Jeremiah 1:10). So what has He called you to build? What industry are you supposed to influence? Where is your business supposed to be operating? What people are you called to reach, serve?

Prior to him returning to Heaven, Jesus gave the disciples a strategic plan – with specific target markets identified – to reach the various people groups of the world (Acts 1:8):

✓ **Jerusalem**: reaching those nearby who were like them.
✓ **Judea**: those further away in distance.
✓ **Samaria**: those further away in culture.
✓ **World**: Global, unreached people groups.

Just like Jesus directed the disciples to go to these different groups, your business is meant to reach certain groups of people. The number one motivating factor that will position you to be successful in connecting with the people in these target markets is love.

Love Thy Customer

In the Kingdom of God and in business, relationships are the most important element. Broken down to its most common denominator, the Bible is a book about the eternal relationship between God and people, and how people are supposed to relate to one another. If you break business down to its most common denominator, the key success factor still comes down to building strong relationships.

God passionately loves people. Therefore, we should passionately love people. God invested His most valuable asset to redeem humanity and reconcile us back to Him. (Side note: In our society we use the words redemption and reconciliation in financial contexts, which gives you an idea of how closely related the Kingdom and business are.). Kingdom entrepreneurs get the privilege and opportunity to love people through your business. As mentioned earlier in this book, your business is an answer to somebody's prayer. But it's not just that. Your business is also an answer to the call to serve.

Love is not often associated with doing business. However, when you serve people through your creativity, ingenuity, quality, and excellence, you are demonstrating love through your business. God sees your investment of time, talent, and resources and will honor your efforts.

$$\langle\langle\langle\diamond\rangle\rangle\rangle$$

B.I.G. Idea:
You can serve without loving, but you can't love without serving.

$$\langle\langle\langle\diamond\rangle\rangle\rangle$$

Business gives Christians the opportunity to use your God-given gifts strategically and purposefully to help others. First Peter 4:10-11 reads, *"God has given gifts to each of you from his great variety of spiritual gifts. Use them well to serve one another... Do it with all the strength and energy that God supplies. Then everything you do will bring glory to God through Jesus Christ..."* (NLT). When Kingdom businesspeople allow God's generosity to flow through you as you exercise your gifts in the marketplace, you are able to have a positive impact on every life that you have the opportunity to touch. Even more, you become fulfilled in your purpose here on the earth when you enhance another's life with your endowed uniqueness.

In this day and time so many businesses seem to no longer value excellent customer service. The reality is they don't understand the blessings promised by God when we love the people He created. When you serve people with a great deal of care and concern, you greatly increase the potential of them moving from just being customers to becoming raving fans.

Don't fall into this society's trap of thinking that love has no place in your business. In fact it is absolutely essential to the success of your business. When you love people God's way, your reward will be earthly and eternal.

Loving your customers is not random or haphazard. It is very strategic. It is planned and executed through branding, marketing, and sales.

Branding, Marketing, and Sales

Many people get confused and think branding, marketing, and sales are all the same when in reality they are not. They are all related, but they each play a very distinct role in your business. To grow a strong business you need to understand how they are distinct from one another and how they work together. The beauty is when these are running like a well-oiled machine, you will be able to turn prospects into customers and customers into loyal, raving fans.

What is Branding?

The identity, image, impact, and impression you create - intentionally and unintentionally - that accurately and passionately represents your organization to the world. Your brand is your story - past, present, and future. It is an actuality of who you are as an organization, as well as a high aspiration of who you desire to become. Your brand communicates your passion. And the essence of your brand should easily be experienced in your mission statement, logo, conversations, blog posts, social media posts, emails, web site, newsletter, videos, transactional experiences, and everything else that is connected to your business.

The truth is everything you do positively or negatively affects your brand. People are always watching. What do they see when they see your business?

The word of God makes it clear in many scriptures what our brand as Christ followers should be, but I think Matthew 5:14-16 sums it up best. *"You are the light of the world. A city set on a hill cannot be hidden... In the same way, let your light shine before others, so that they may see your good works and give glory to your Father who is in heaven."* Our lives as Christians should ignite a hunger in people to want a relationship with God. Our life brand should cause people to look through us to see Jesus.

The essential thing to remember about your brand is the lasting impression that people are left with when you are not around to explain you or your company. Your company's brand represents your business's character or reputation. It can take a long time to develop, but just one unfortunate incident to tear it down.

Do not take lightly the intentional time, thought, and focus that is required to build and become a long-standing brand that is respected and even loved.

<<<❖>>>

B.I.G. Idea:
Your brand is the mental real estate that you occupy in people's minds.

<<<❖>>>

As you begin to develop your branding strategy, the first question you must ask is, *"Who is your customer?"* This is a fundamental question that most entrepreneurs don't spend enough time defining. Although we would all like to think that everyone in the world will want the amazing things that we create and sell, that is the furthest thing from the reality of the marketplace. According to my friend Patrice Tsague, co-founder and Chief Servant Officer of Nehemiah Project International Ministries, he says, *"Everybody is not your customer. Anybody is not your customer. Somebody is your customer."* The key is defining your "somebody," which I will help you do shortly.

The second fundamental question you must ask in relation to building your brand is *"What do they want?"* You must be able to identify a problem, need, or desire within your target market for which your business has the passion and ability to provide a cost-effective solution. Creating products and services that are only based on your interests is the quickest way to fail in business. The thing that will guarantee you staying in business is continually solving problems, meeting needs, and satisfying desires better and more consistently than other businesses.

When you try to brand your business to appease everyone, you usually end up appeasing no one. Generally speaking, customers today are more discerning with their spending habits, so most people would rather pay for a specialist than a generalist. What's the difference between a specialist and a generalist? Generalists have a lot of information and ideas for a broad audience, but specialists have specific solutions for specific target markets. Businesses with strong brands understand they must decide where and how they are going to specialize that will allow them to have the greatest long-term revenue potential.

I will discuss this topic of becoming a specialist more in the next chapter. For now let's move on to talk about marketing.

What is Marketing?
Marketing is the intentional and thorough process of finding out what customers want, then engaging in specific activities to meet their needs in ways that can produce a profit. Marketing is how you communicate your brand to the world. Marketing includes market research, deciding on products and prices, advertising, promotion, and distribution. From a Kingdom perspective, it is very similar in function to evangelism.

Marketing is crucially important to a business, because it sets the stage for sales. Marketing creates a desire for your product or service; sales closes the deal. Again, from my friend Patrice Tsague: *"Marketing plants the seeds, sales reaps the harvest."*

Your marketing strategy is critical aspect of the execution of your mission. Without an effective marketing strategy to acquire customers and generate revenues, you will not build a profitable or sustainable business.

Marketing Pillars

The basic concept of marketing is very simple. It essentially comes down to identifying what people want and delivering it to them. The implementation of this simple premise can sometimes be challenging. Being able to easily answer the following questions (4Ps) will help you clarify your marketing strategy:

⇨ **Product**: What do you sell?

⇨ **Place**: Where do you sell it?

⇨ **Price**: How much do you sell it for?

⇨ **Promotion**: How do you let customers know what you're selling?

Effective marketing is both art and science, so you need to have clarity in these four areas in order to develop and execute a winning strategy.

Develop Desirable Product and Service Solutions

The first rule of entrepreneurship is to find a need and fill it. So no matter what type of business you are in, you cannot create solutions in a vacuum. Your solutions must be easily attractive to your target customers based on their need that you are filling or the problem you are solving. Marketing helps you identify your customer's needs and problems, as well as what your competitors are doing. Here are four questions you can ask yourself about whether your solution exceeds what is already in the marketplace:

1) **Is it faster?**: Your solution is faster than other solutions that already exist.

2) **Is it better?**: Your solution provides your customers with a high quality solution or better experience than what is currently in the marketplace.

3) **Is it cheaper?**: You help your customer make more money or save more money than what already exists.

4) **Is it easier?**: You help your customer do things more efficiently, i.e. get more things done in less amount of time.

If your solution does not surpass your competition in one or more of these areas it will be very hard for it to gain traction with customers, because they will not have an incentive to switch. Only when you are able to answer the 4P questions above and have a solution that exceeds your competition, are you ready to move into sales. If you don't have these questions answered first it will make your sales job extremely challenging.

What is Sales?

Many people have misconceptions about sales and are turned off, mainly because of bad experiences with salespeople. The truth is every entrepreneur is a salesperson, whether you like sales or not. So here is a simple definition of sales to help you get rid of the bad taste that this word may leave in your mouth.

Selling is simply offering something of value to someone that they need or desire. So what are you offering? The answer is value. Providing value means efficiently and effectively satisfying a customer's needs, issues, or desires in a manner that is cost agreeable for the customer. When you look at sales from that perspective, you should be excited to offer your products or services to prospective customers. However, if you have trouble defining what your value is, then sales will be difficult.

Key Question: How do you know what your customers consider valuable?

Discovering Your Opportunities

To determine how you are going to meet a customer's needs, issues or desires, you must first be able to determine what they are and how what you do aligns. This is the opportunity that is waiting to be discovered. You must become an expert at identifying and evaluating your target market's hopes, dreams, expectations, frustrations, habits, tendencies, etc. Some people call this psychographics. Marketing techniques that leverage this type of information are being used more often today, even by politicians to help them project how people are going to vote.

The reason knowing this information is so important is that successful product and service ideas need to connect with your customer in at least five distinct ways, which are in essence decision gateways. These gateways are the criteria that your customers will use to choose your solution or another company's. They include:

1) **Operational**: Performs the desired function.
2) **Technical**: Meets the desired specifications.
3) **Financial**: Fits reasonably within the budget.
4) **Practical**: Ease of use.
5) **Emotional**: Mental satisfaction.

As you go through this list you must consider how you will use these gateways to prove to your customer that you have the right solution for their problem. Many entrepreneurs get caught up in overloading their customer prospects with facts and features. However, if you look at this list, features only address operational and technical concerns. Well, another sales philosophy says to focus on the benefits of your offering. Yet, that still falls short of incorporating all the connection points identified on this list.

The connection point that is often left out by sellers is mental satisfaction. No matter how many features your solution has, how much it costs, or how easy it is to use, all buyers want to have peace of mind that they made the best choice. They want to be confident that they made the right selection and will not suffer remorse because of it. Other examples of positive emotional impact that you want to relay to your customers include happiness, pleasure, stability, security, comfort, excitement, significance, a sense of purpose, and more. You can consider this emotional or psychological capital.

If you spend a good amount of time building emotional capital by crafting your marketing and sales strategies to address the emotional needs of your prospective customers, you will experience much success in attracting them to your products and services.

《《❖》》

B.I.G. Idea:
Opportunities often come disguised as problems.

《《❖》》

You may be wondering is it possible to get access to how your prospective customers think and feel. The answer is yes. We will discuss the different ways to do this in the next chapter. For now let's continue down this path of discovering the opportunity.

Targeting Customer Needs

Early on in your planning process, you must decide whom you want your business to serve and how you want to serve them. Depending on whether your target is other businesses or consumers, you will have a different focus on how to identify and target your customer's needs. First, we will look at businesses and then consumers.

Business Customers

When your target market is other businesses, your product or service must impact one of more of the same five core business functions that you must manage in your own business:

1) People
2) Products & Services
3) Processes
4) Performance Management
5) Profit Management

How does your product or service enhance or improve these areas for your customer? How does your product or service help your customer save or make more money, increase their access to information, or increase their access to resources? How are you going to help that business be more successful?

Consumer Customers

If your main target is consumers, lifestyle quality issues are the areas in which you need to focus on impacting, which would include:

1. Basic survival	6. Recreational
2. Health	7. Spiritual
3. Physical	8. Educational
4. Emotional	9. Financial
5. Mental	10. Relational

Key Question: How does your product or service enhance or improve these areas for your customer? How does your product or service help your customer save or make more money, increase their access to information, increase their access to resources?

Key Question: What is your value proposition? Which of your customer's needs, issues or desires does your product/service impact? How does your product/service improve or enhance your customer's quality of life?

Key Question: In what ways can you measure your product/service's impact on your customer's business performance or quality of life?

Selling vs. Serving

As Kingdom entrepreneurs we must understand there is often a difference between the people to which we sell our products and services versus the people we have been called to serve through our businesses. Many Christians in business make the mistake of trying to sell their products and services to the people they have a desire or passion to serve. Unfortunately, this produces unintended consequences.

Often times the people you're called to serve can't afford to give you the necessary value for what you have created. That then causes you to struggle to generate sufficient income because your sales will be low or you wrongly assume you shouldn't deal with them altogether because you aren't generating enough revenues. The issue is not that you shouldn't deal with them. The issue is that you had them in the wrong category. You mistakenly tried to sell to the people you were called to serve.

I recently heard the story of a real estate developer whose business model is selling unique, high-end, multi-million dollar homes to the ultra-rich. He then uses the profits from his successful business to serve the ultra-poor. He clearly understands his calling to serve people, by using a profitable business model directed toward customers who can fully afford to pay for what he sells. If you already recognize the people God called you to serve, ask Him to whom you should sell your products and services so that your business can grow profitably and you can then use your profits to bless those others.

CHAPTER 10

PRICING AND POSITIONING

"For which of you, desiring to build a tower, does not first sit down and
count the cost, whether he has enough to complete it?"
Luke 14:28

V-STAR BUSINESS PLANNING SYSTEM

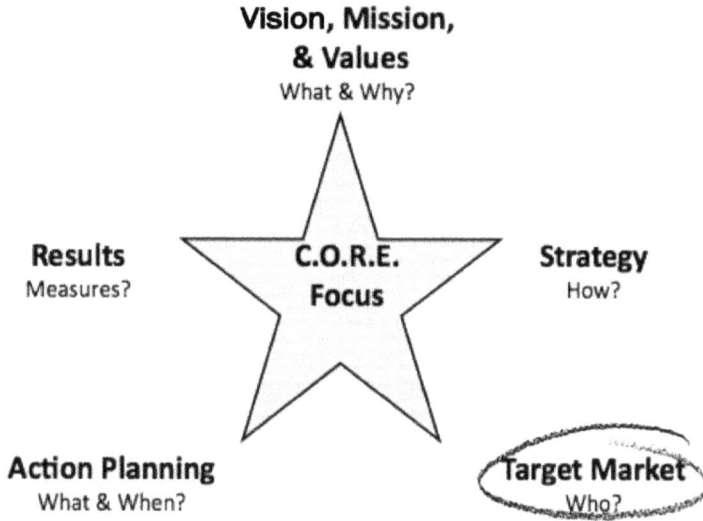

Vision, Mission, & Values
What & Why?

Results
Measures?

C.O.R.E. Focus

Strategy
How?

Action Planning
What & When?

Target Market
Who?

Financial Sustainability

I am sure you have probably heard people talk about the necessity and benefits of having multiple streams of income. There is Biblical precedent for this concept. In Genesis 2:5-14 we can see how God created the Garden of Eden (and the earth as a whole) to be self-sustaining. He designed four rivers to flow into and out of Eden. One of the things that is really interesting about this impressive irrigation system is the meanings of the names of the rivers. God had you in mind even when he was designing these rivers!

1. **Pishon** means increase.
2. **Gihon** means break forth.
3. **Hiddikel** means rapid.
4. **Euphrates** means fruitfulness.

In the same manner that God designed the earth to be naturally self-sustaining, you must design your business to do the same. No matter which revenue model that you choose, you must develop multiple rivers of income so that you can be sustainable over the long-term. I would suggest that you develop plans for at least four income sources that you create through the development of complementary products and services within your business model.

Creating multiple rivers of income will allow you to have the financial flexibility to weather economic storms. You will be positioned to transfer your efforts to growing other streams when certain ones are not flowing as well. Building additional income sources may not be something that you can do initially, but it is definitely something you want to focus on over the long-term.

⟨⟨⟨❖⟩⟩⟩

B.I.G. Idea:
If God ordained it He will sustain it!

⟨⟨⟨❖⟩⟩⟩

Another aspect of your sustainability is finding the place God has already prepared for you to succeed. Each of the tribes of Israel was given specific geographic regions of land as their inheritance (except the Levites). Likewise, God has set aside territories in which you will prosper, which are actually specific groups of people He wants you to reach and impact for the Kingdom. These would be your target markets or industry niches. God has already carved out your path to success, so it should be of no concern to you what other businesses are doing even if there are similarities. He might even call you to start an industry does not yet exist. You can call your chosen space to flourish Rehoboth, which means "God has given us room enough" (Genesis 26:22). Claim your territory and ask God how He wants you to impact people's lives.

The most critical factor that will allow your business to be sustained in the place where God has called you to succeed is obedience to His directives. And this includes adherence to how you are supposed to incorporate the spiritual and social elements related to the "Triple Bottom Line" introduced earlier in this book. You must be careful not to just focus on your financial bottom line and neglect the other two. As a Kingdom CEO, God is going to hold you accountable for all three.

Triple Bottom Line

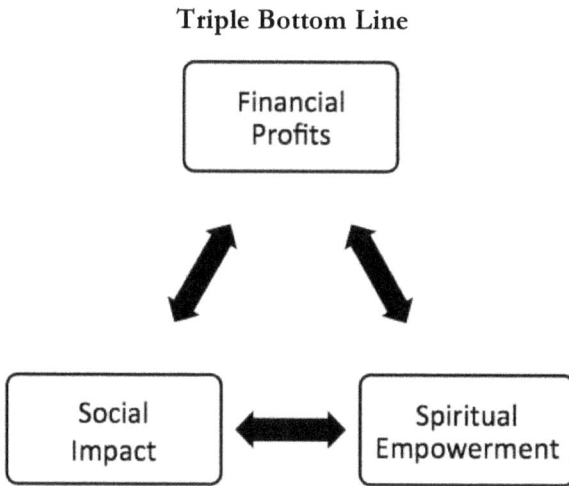

There are Riches in the Niches

Conventional business wisdom says you should look for the largest customer groups possible to market your products and services in order to generate sustainable income. However, sometimes the greatest value can be found in the unlikeliest of places. Those places are often hidden inside smaller customer niches. In your business, going against conventional wisdom and developing narrow clusters of loyal, repeat customers may result in your biggest breakthroughs.

So what is a niche and how do you determine which one to target? A niche is a specifically defined segment of customers in the marketplace. Niches are usually subsets or micro-segments of the broader market, and are delineated by an intersection of shared characteristics, such as age, gender, income, geography, profession, religious preferences, aspirations, political affiliations, and more. Examples that you may be familiar with are terms used by political groups such as "soccer moms" or "NASCAR dads." These titles sound simple, but they are undergirded by a lot of research that categorizes groups of people that share many similar characteristics.

You can define a niche in almost any way you want to. However, you have to determine if the niche you define can be profitable for your business. Within that group of people must exist a measurable financial capacity, spending power, and a desire for your products or services, else you will be wasting your time and energy.

In terms of strategic positioning, I have come to believe in the business philosophy that you first go deep in a niche and then grow wide. When you are able to find an existing niche where you can have great influence or define a new niche where you can dominate, you are opening up your business to untold opportunities.

Going Deep

Going deep in a niche means you have a profitable means of strategically focusing on becoming the "go-to" company for new products, information, ideas, insights, innovation, and expertise for a targeted group of customers. It necessitates that you shape your branding, marketing, and sales strategies specifically for your target market. Your efforts are very intentional and concentrated rather than broad or random, resulting in a funnel effect. You will be more profitable by delivering significant value as a specialist focused on the needs, challenges, and desires of that group instead of as a generalist who demonstrates only a broad understanding of the group but not an expertise. The more you know about a niche the more you can dominate your competitors.

Marketing Funnel

Number of Target Customers Decreases as Your Focus Increases

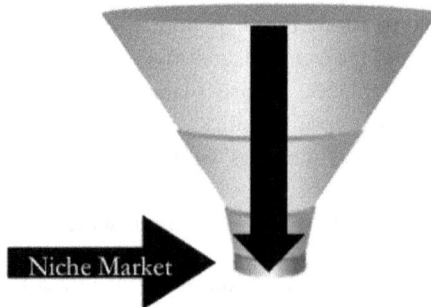

Niche Market

Once you have defined your target niche and determined that it's financially beneficial to pursue, the next step is to ask two key questions about your niche:

1) What are their interests, cares, concerns, and needs (expressed or implied)?
2) How does the combination of my passion and expertise connect with their interests, cares, concerns, needs, etc.?

Next, you must position your company as the expert for this target audience and determine how you will serve them. Your entire focus has to be on creating value for them. As an expert you must create solutions that connect with your target niche's communicated need or desire. You can do this in one of the two following ways:

1) Create a core product/service solution for multiple related niches.
   OR
2) Create multiple product/service solution for a specific niche.

The goal is to be able to build a strong, loyal following of paying customers in your target niche(s). Their loyalty is defined by their repeat purchases and willingness to share their positive experience with others. These customer testimonials become an inexpensive but vital part of your marketing strategy to new customers.

Once your core offering(s) is successful you are now positioned to go deeper into your niche. From this point two strategic options you have are:

1) Create additional product/service solutions for your core niche(s).
   OR
2) Market your current solutions to other related niches.

You must continue the process that I discussed earlier in terms of determining needs, addressing concerns, focusing on serving At the point where your participants, popularity, and profits begin to grow in your niche, I call it "flipping the funnel." This allows you to expand your customer base, which can significantly increase your company's profit potential the deeper you work into your target niche market.

Some entrepreneurs are fearful of pursuing niche markets, because they think they might miss out on opportunities in other niches. My first counterpoint is you can't let fear drive your decision-making. Knowing the market God has called you to target gives you confidence in making the best decisions. Secondly, for your long-term sustainability you have to build a loyal customer following. It's much more difficult to do that across many customer groups that are dissimilar versus building strong ties within smaller segments that share similarities.

"Flipping the Funnel"

**Number of Target Customers
Decreases as Focus Increases**

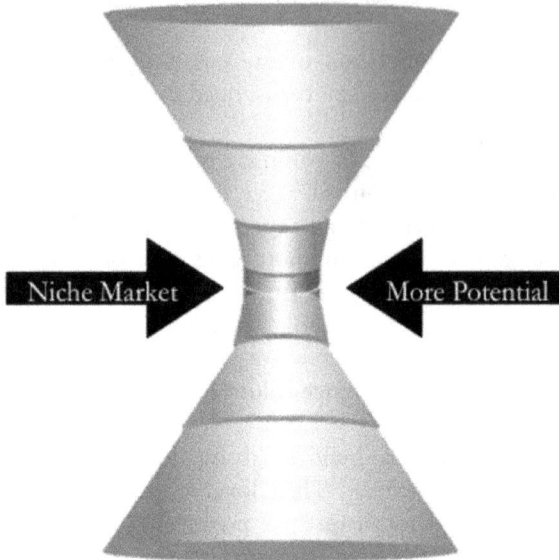

**Number of Loyal Customers Increases as You Build
Brand Value and Increase Solutions**

The whole point of going deeper in a niche is to continue to create value with your solutions that cause current customers to increase their loyalty through additional revenues while you are constantly attracting new customers. Let's look at a couple of simple examples:

Niche Level	Software Company	Business Consultant	Consumer Product
Tier 1: Free or Basic offering	Free 30 day trial	Free evaluation or report	Buy 1, Get 1 free
Tier 2: Standard solution	Standard product	Training workshop	Standard product
Tier 3: Customized solution	Custom software development	Individual consulting engagement	Specialized, unique design

In order for this process to become most profitable, you must position your solutions at the appropriate price points for your niche.

Pricing and Positioning

One of the most difficult things to do in business is deciding what price to charge for your solutions. You must determine how to provide the greatest value to your customers efficiently, effectively, and profitably based on the revenue model that is most appropriate for your target customer.

Your pricing strategy and market positioning is largely determined by your revenue model. A revenue model helps you identify and narrow down the type of customer you want to serve and the price points you will need to utilize.

What is your Revenue Model?

Your pricing strategy and market positioning is largely determined by your revenue model. A revenue model helps you identify and narrow down the type of customer you want to serve and the price points you will need to utilize. Another way to think about your revenue model is how your product/service intersects with customer preferences and their buying behaviors. This includes how they evaluate the critical of the need of the solution in comparison to the price point.

Four Basic Revenue Models

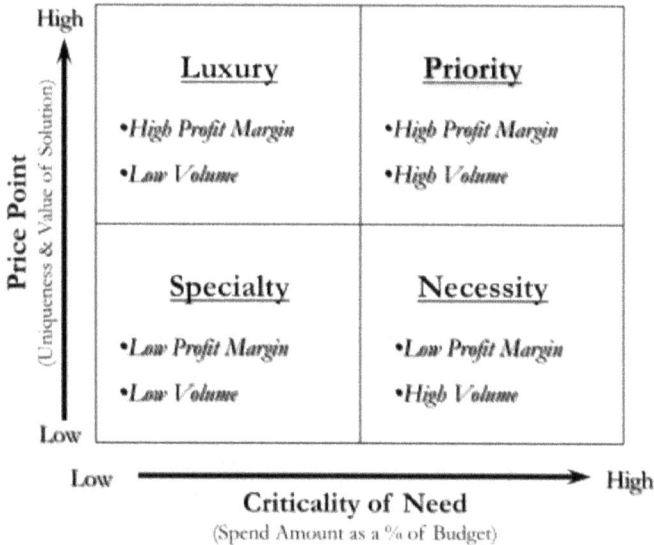

	High	
	Luxury	**Priority**
	•*High Profit Margin*	•*High Profit Margin*
Price Point (Uniqueness & Value of Solution)	•*Low Volume*	•*High Volume*
	Specialty	**Necessity**
	•*Low Profit Margin*	•*Low Profit Margin*
	•*Low Volume*	•*High Volume*
	Low	

Low ⟶ High

Criticality of Need
(Spend Amount as a % of Budget)

As you identify the appropriate revenue model for your business you will be able to discover and leverage competitive advantages to position you build a strong customer base. The table on the next page provides an explanation for each market position.

Revenue Model Characteristics

Quadrant	Characteristics	Examples
I. Necessity	<ul><li>High volume, low-cost leader</li><li>Many customers</li><li>Low profit margins</li><li>Many competitors</li><li>Many product or service alternatives</li><li>Benefits of economies of scale</li></ul>	Wal-Mart Grocery stores Household goods
II. Specialty	<ul><li>Niche player</li><li>Fewer customers</li><li>Low profit margins</li><li>Many sources</li><li>Little product differentiation</li></ul>	Dollar stores Promotional products Virtual assistant
III. Luxury	<ul><li>Highly specialized products or services</li><li>High-end (specialty)</li><li>Fewer customers</li><li>Fewer competitors</li><li>Fewer customers</li><li>High profit margins</li></ul>	Luxury clothing Apple Coaching Info products
IV. Priority	<ul><li>Suppliers offer unique capabilities</li><li>Price is not the primary consideration</li><li>Impact on business is critical</li><li>Many competitors</li><li>Many customers</li></ul>	Auto Dealer Travel Computers Smart phones
V. Blended	Combination of multiple models	Technology Construction Consulting

It is crucial for you to understand that no company can be all things to all customers. You must determine the best revenue model for your company as it relates to your customers' preferences and behaviors. You also have to consider what your customer considers as critical versus non-critical in their budget. Just because you believe it's critical does not mean they will. That's why it's so important to know what those in your target niche consider as critical.

Find your target niche and develop your products and services to be the best solution for those customers. The more you understand about your niche the more you can dominate it. When you narrow your focus on the right niche for you, your business can explode with opportunities!

《《✦》》

B.I.G. Idea:

Do not try to be all things to all customers at the same time. Find a niche and stick to it. There are riches in the niches!

《《✦》》

Barriers to Entry and Exit

Every industry has barriers or requirements that you must be able to satisfy in order to start and grow your business. Obviously, some industries have higher barriers to get in than others. The greater the barriers the more difficult it will be or the longer it will take to get started in your industry. On the other hand, the simpler the barriers the easier or quicker it will be to get start in your industry. Some of these barriers could include:

- ✓ Large capital investment
- ✓ Real estate, including land or buildings
- ✓ Licenses
- ✓ Certifications
- ✓ Regulatory requirements
- ✓ Governmental requirements
- ✓ Inventory
- ✓ Insurance and bonding requirements
- ✓ Membership fees
- ✓ Others

It's important that you research your industry to find out the startup and operating requirements that have been established by different legal or regulatory bodies, including local, state, federal, or other official entities.

Barriers to exit are similar to barriers to entry in that they determine how hard it is to get out of the business. More than likely if it was hard to get into the business, it will not be that easy to get out of it. There may be special requirements, such as how you legally dissolve the business, how you are to dispose of assets, and how long you're supposed to keep certain records. Again, check with industry trade groups and experts to get a better understanding of the exit requirements, which will serve to keep you out of trouble down the line.

Strategic Considerations

An important benefit of identifying your revenue model is recognizing the opportunities and limitations of your solutions. For example, is your solution a Necessity or Priority item for your targeted niche? Is your solution a Specialty or Luxury? How your target niche views your product or service will determine your long-term revenue potential based on their buying preferences and behaviors.

Of course every entrepreneur would like to think their business falls into the Strategic category, which has a high price point and high criticality factor. However, that is not reality. The better you understand your target niche, the better you will be a to implement a profitable revenue model for your business.

A big factor that will determine which revenue model you can operate with profitably has to do with revenue model barriers. These are different than the industry related entry/exit barriers I wrote about earlier in this chapter. These particular barriers are the revenue model requirements that need to be met in order for you to compete in each space. The reality is in many niches it's hard to initially be considered as a Luxury or Strategic solution. However, if you continue to produce value for your customers you can reposition yourself in a different revenue model within that niche.

Determine where you want your business to be in the long-term, so that even if you start off with a revenue model that has lower profit margins today you can grow it to higher profit margins in the future. The more you increase your value, the more you will increase your profits.

〈〈〈❖〉〉〉

B.I.G. Idea:
Determine where you want to be in the long-term.
The more you increase your value the more you will increase your profits.

〈〈〈❖〉〉〉

Revenue Model Strategic Considerations

Revenue Model	Barrier Difficulty	Strategic Considerations
Priority	High	• Harder to get in, but it's also harder to find a replacement for you if you do well. • More expertise is required. • Products/services are usually more complex. • Customer loyalty is very strong.
Luxury	High	• Continue to create a dependency that makes it harder to replace you the longer the relationship goes on. • Focus on acquiring/advancing: Licenses, certifications, education, specialty skills, experience, expertise, capital, facilities, size, other
Necessity	Low	• Easier to get in, but it's also easier for customers to find a replacement for you. • Customer loyalty is weak. • FUD Factor ("Fear, Uncertainty, and Doubt") – Create a sense of urgency that helps position you closer to Luxury or Priority. • Get in through a low barrier, but attempt to transition to another position.
Specialty	Low	

Key Questions:
How would you define your revenue model?

What key factors led you to choose that revenue model?

What are the key barriers to entry and exit for your chosen revenue model?

What are four revenue streams that you can develop with your product or service?

1)

2)

3)

4)

Business Basics

At the beginning of the chapter we discussed the Biblical concept of sustainability. For every Biblical truth there are corresponding practical actions. The goal of any business that wants to stay in business is to maximize profits, which is done in two main ways: 1) increasing income and 2) decreasing expenses. It is amazing how many entrepreneurs go out of business because they ignore these two basic principles that are applicable no matter how big or small your business is.

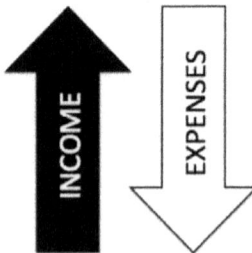

Increasing Income

Income = Selling Price x Quantity

If you ask any successful entrepreneur, growing your income streams is both parts art and science. As you can see from the income equation, it's very easy to understand. Nevertheless, most business owners will have to use some combination of income growth strategies, but to some degree they will all include...

⇨ Increasing your number of customers
⇨ Increasing your sales volume per customer
⇨ Increasing your prices on current products
⇨ Introducing products with higher prices

Initially this may seem like trial and error, but you can use a tool that I call a Pricing Funnel to help you sort it out.

Pricing Funnel

With every pricing strategy, you must be aware of your market positioning with your target customers and the corresponding pricing strategy that is best targeted to them. Lower prices are usually associated with the Necessity and Specialty product/service categories, while higher prices usually fall within the Priority and Luxury categories.

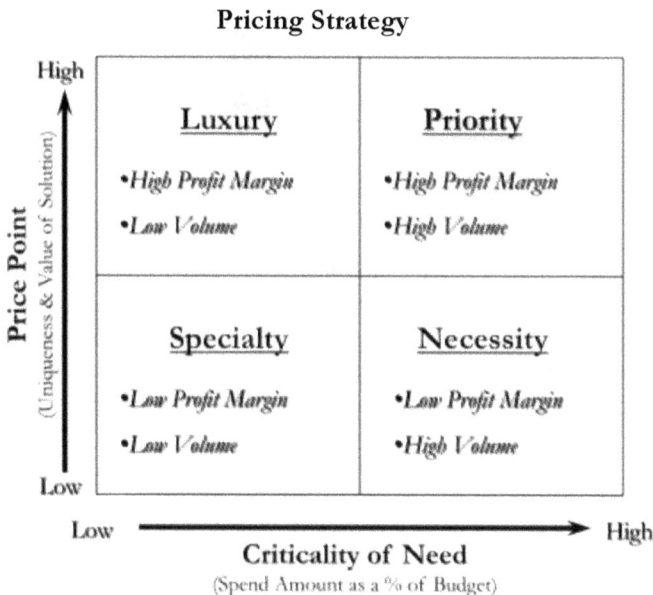

Pricing Strategy

	Luxury	**Priority**
High	•*High Profit Margin* •*Low Volume*	•*High Profit Margin* •*High Volume*
	Specialty	**Necessity**
Low	•*Low Profit Margin* •*Low Volume*	•*Low Profit Margin* •*High Volume*

Price Point
(Uniqueness & Value of Solution)

Low ⟶ High

Criticality of Need
(Spend Amount as a % of Budget)

A pricing funnel is a range of products for your niche that have different price points. The thought is that the lower price points, often starting with free, will attract a large number of interested customers. And the longer they stay connected to you the more products and services that you can introduce at increasing intervals.

The funneling aspect of this is the higher you go in price the more narrow your funnel becomes because customers opt out at their chosen price ceiling. However, what should also be happening is that as you introduce higher priced products in the marketplace, particularly to your target niche, your profits and profit margins will increase. So your revenues from the higher priced solutions should outpace the siphoning of customers. Your profitability will grow as you go deeper into your niche and wider in your solution offerings.

Pricing Funnel

Number of Customers

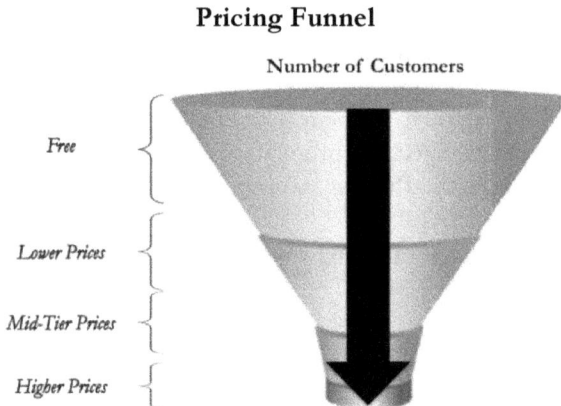

Free

Lower Prices

Mid-Tier Prices

Higher Prices

One key benefit of this approach to pricing is that you can create a mix of customers at different price points so that you are not solely dependent upon one product or one customer group to drive all of your revenues. You can consider this a diversified customer portfolio approach. Also, this is a very effective strategy for transitioning customers from lower priced solutions to higher priced solutions over time.

Pricing Funnel + Increasing Profitability

Number of Customers

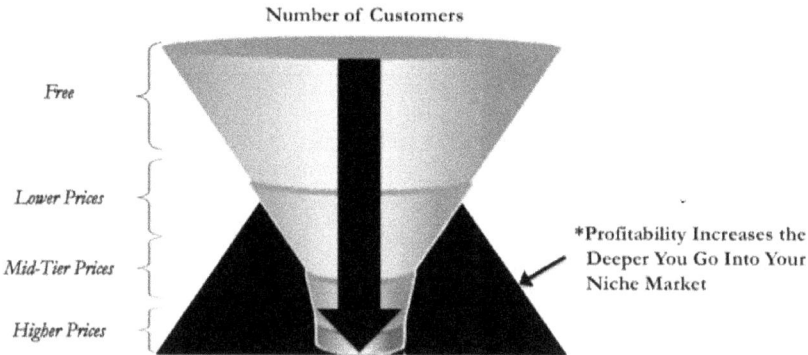

Free

Lower Prices

Mid-Tier Prices

Higher Prices

*Profitability Increases the Deeper You Go Into Your Niche Market

One caveat to this approach is that if you get too caught up in trying to create a product for every tier, your company could come off as trying to cater to too many different audiences. To avoid that trap use this funnel within you chosen niche to drive prospects from one solution to the next as the value increases for what they receive at those higher price points.

Pricing Considerations
⇨ Revisit your marketing strategy map for products/services.
⇨ Assess your customer base to ensure your price point fits your customer profile.
⇨ Review your product/pricing mix – which could mean you need to implement tiered pricing, i.e. a different level of prices for different solutions.
⇨ Ask yourself is it easier for you to get a new customer or grow your sales volume with current customers?

Customer Profitability Analysis
As you are going through this process you may be asking yourself how will you know if you have the chosen the right customer niche or solution/pricing mix. That is a great question. It is very important to understand how well each of your solutions is performing as well as how well you are doing in each target market in which you are doing business. The Customer Profitability Analysis explains the profit and loss per customer for each of your target markets or products categories (see sample on the next page). You do not have to use this exact tool, but something similar will be very beneficial to you as you analysis and assess which customer niches and products/services are going to be most profitable for you.

Sample Customer Profitability Analysis
Kingdom Business, Inc.
2010 - 2013

	Training Materials	Software	Consulting	Overall
Customer Activity:				
Number of active customers—Beginning of period	10	8	8	26
Number of customers added	37	29	10	76
Number of customers lost/terminated	(3)	(3)	(1)	(7)
Number of active customers—End of period	44	34	17	95
Profitability Analysis:				
Revenue per segment	$970,000	$2,500,000	$1,800,000	$5,270,000
Weighting	18.4%	47.4%	34.2%	100.0%
Cost of sales:				
Ongoing service and support costs	$100,000	$1,400,000	$350,000	$1,850,000
Other direct customer costs	200,000	100,000	100,000	400,000
Total cost of sales	$300,000	$1,500,000	$450,000	$2,250,000
Gross margin	$670,000	$1,000,000	$1,350,000	$3,020,000
Weighting	22.2%	33.1%	44.7%	100.0%
Other costs:				
Customer acquisition	$105,000	$120,000	$235,000	$460,000
Customer marketing	150,000	125,000	275,000	550,000
Customer termination	80,000	190,000	140,000	410,000
Total other customer costs	$335,000	$435,000	$650,000	$1,420,000
Customer profit by segment	$335,000	$565,000	$700,000	$1,600,000
Weighting	20.9%	35.3%	43.8%	100.0%

Summary Metrics:	Training Materials	Software	Consulting
Average cost per acquired customer	$2,838	$4,138	$23,500
Average cost per terminated customer	$26,667	$63,333	$140,000
Average marketing cost per active customer	$3,409	$3,676	$16,176
Average profit (loss) per customer	$7,614	$16,618	$41,176

Summary Metrics Per Customer Segment

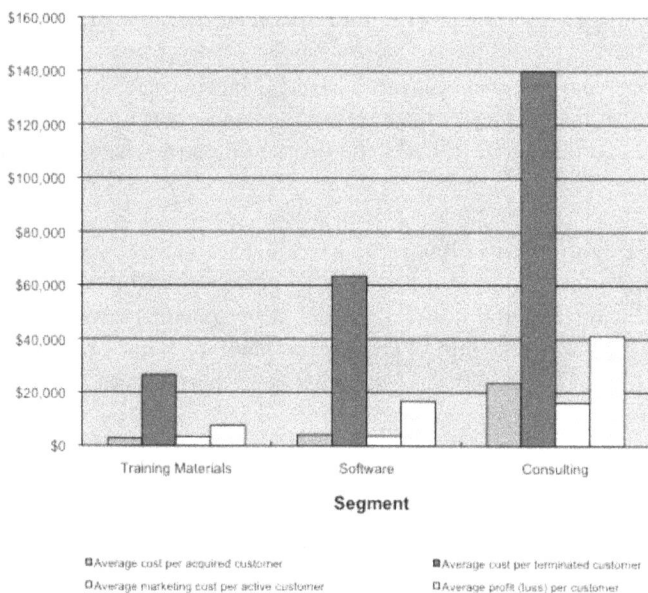

Two things that will have a great influence on your customer profitability are your product/service management and customer relationship management. Here are some suggestions that will help you maximize your profitability in these two areas:

1) Product/Service Management
- ✓ Goal: Deliver high quality products/services that consistently meet your customers' needs or desires.
- ✓ Closely align your sales/revenue goals with your company vision and values.
- ✓ Focus on building a brand known for great quality.
- ✓ Monitor and measure results at consistent intervals.

2) Customer Relationship Management
- ✓ Goal: Build customer loyalty.
- ✓ Closely align customer service goals with your company vision and values.
- ✓ Focus on relationship building, by providing a high quality experience.

- ✓ Solicit continuous feedback from customers (formal and informal).
- ✓ Incorporate feedback into products/services.
- ✓ Manage expectations, i.e. under-promise and over-deliver.

In a later chapter dealing with Results Management we will discuss additional tools that you can utilize to monitor and measure your marketing performance, so that you can make the proper adjustments to maximize the ROI of your efforts.

Don't Stay Beyond Your Grace

When things are going well it is easy to get comfortable. However, you have to be aware that the conditions that allowed you to succeed are not always going to stay the same. The marketplace is always changing, new competitors are always coming, and customer preferences could change unexpectedly.

God's grace was on the Israelites while Joseph was alive. It was reflected in their residence in Goshen, which was the best land in Egypt for animals and growing crops (Genesis 45:18, 47:6). However, years later after the death of Joseph a new Pharaoh came into office that did not know who Joseph was. And when he looked around and saw how the number of Israelites had grown exponentially, he now viewed them as a threat instead of an asset and decided to enslave them. What started out as a blessing for Jacob's family turned into curse just a couple of generations later.

As an entrepreneur you must recognize when the grace of God is present where you are and when it has left. This could relate to your involvement with certain target markets, business relationships, product lines, industries, etc. When God's grace is present you will prosper. But when God declares a season to be over and His grace leaves that relationship, situation, or opportunity, if you stay in the same place you will be forced to do things in your own strength, which will eventually lead to frustration, fruitlessness, and failure. Don't get left behind when God is on the move!

CHAPTER 11

MOBILIZE MY MARKETING

"… I have become all things to all people, that by all means
I might save some."
1 Corinthians 9:22

V-STAR BUSINESS PLANNING SYSTEM

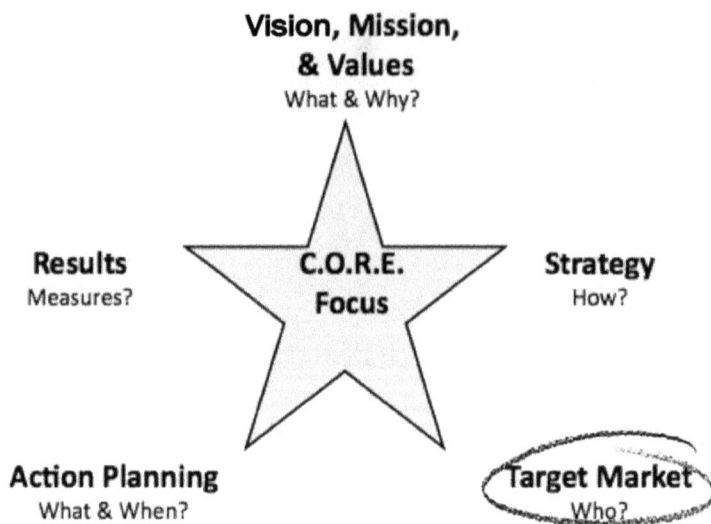

**Vision, Mission,
& Values**
What & Why?

Results
Measures?

**C.O.R.E.
Focus**

Strategy
How?

Action Planning
What & When?

Target Market
Who?

Seed, Time, and Harvest

In this chapter we are going to discuss developing and executing your marketing plan. To get started I want to present a foundational Kingdom business principle that will accelerate your marketing efforts.

Building a successful and sustainable Kingdom business requires long-term, proactive thinking, not just knee-jerk reactions to news and fads happening in the marketplace. God, in His infinite wisdom, created a universal principle that works in nature as well as in business called "Seed, Time, and Harvest." Let's explore how this Biblical principle applies to your business, specifically as it relates to building and marketing your brand.

Strong brands that evoke enthusiastic customer loyalty are built over time not all at once. They are fashioned piece by piece like a puzzle. Each piece has a cumulative effect that adds positively to what's already in place.

Enthusiastic customer loyalty is nurtured through repeated consistent, high-quality experiences from the products and services they invest in. Quality and consistency can't be established with one idea or campaign. Companies with strong brands understand this.

Yes, there are times when individual marketing activities have a big impact, however, strong brands do not get intoxicated by that and rest on their laurels. They keep working on incorporating the next pieces that will allow them to extend and sustain their influence, so they are not just be a flash in the pan.

This approach reminds me of a scented candle. It does not burn fast like a match, but eventually its aroma fills an entire room. You do not want a "brand scent" that burns brightly for a short while, but then is quickly forgotten about. You want your brand to leave a pleasant aroma with your customers that lingers for a long time. Seed, time, and harvest may not always be fast, but it is effective.

⟨⟨⟨❖⟩⟩⟩

B.I.G. Idea:
Seed, time, and harvest may not always be fast, but it is effective.

⟨⟨⟨❖⟩⟩⟩

Paradigm of the Sower

God understands marketing better than anyone else, because He has been doing it the longest. In Mark 4:1-20, Jesus does a superb job of giving us a framework of what types of people entrepreneurs will engage in the marketplace in terms of their willingness and readiness to purchase your product. Let's explore some key learnings from the Parable of the Sower.

Before you continue reading make sure you read these verses so that you can understand the context of this discussion.

To paraphrase this parable, while in a large crowd Jesus told a story about a farmer who went out to sow seeds along a path and the different types of terrain that his seeds fell on, including the side of the path, stony ground, thorny ground, and fertile ground. Later that day when he was alone with his disciples Jesus interpreted his words for them. He explained that the seeds on the side of the path were God's word that had fallen in the shallow places of a person's heart that is easily stolen by the devil. He revealed that the stony ground represents those who allow affliction or offense to deplete the word from their lives. He then said that the thorns represented those who allowed the deceitfulness of riches, cares of the world and the lust for things other than God to choke out the fruitfulness of the word. Lastly, Jesus describes how those who hear the word and receive it produce various levels of increasing fruitfulness.

The paradigm entrepreneurs must embrace is that this parable closely resembles the opportunities and challenges you will face in the marketplace in terms of marketing and selling your products. When you are transacting in the marketplace you will interact with some people who completely disregard what you are offering without any consideration. You will have others who may initially seem interested, but then different challenges get in the way of them making a decision. There will be another group of people who will go along with you for a while, but then allow distractions or other options to keep them from following through on a purchase with you. The last group consists of those on which you want to focus most of your attention. These are the people who "get it" and are willing to move forward with you to make a transaction and build a relationship. You will reap your greatest harvest from people who truly understand the value that you offer is the solution to their need.

Do not waste valuable time trying to convince people they need what you have. Continuing with the farmer analogy, some people are in the fall or winter season of their decision making process and all you can really do is plant and nurture seeds that could be harvested in the future. Other people are in the spring decision cycle just need some more coaxing to make a decision. Those in the summer season are ready now for you to close the deal. As you recognize where people are you will be able to judge how much time to spend with them.

3 Keys to Biblical Marketing

Here are three keys to consider with this Biblical approach to marketing for your Kingdom business:
1) **Strategic**: Consider every new tip and tool within the confines of your current strategy and budget. As you add new things make sure

they complement what you're already doing. If you feel the need to do something radical, reconsider your entire strategy not just one piece of it.

2) **Significant**: Every marketing effort should have either an immediate or cumulative measurable benefit.

3) **Sustainable**: Make sure that whatever you do is not a one-shot deal, but something that you can do continually and consistently well.

I have to admit this methodical approach runs counter to our make-a-fast-buck culture. I also have to admit that I sometimes get frustrated when I see other companies that seem to be making a bigger splash than I am and creating more buzz. Nevertheless, we must realize that we are building for the long haul and what we do today may not produce immediate dividends, but we will reap the rewards in the long run.

Seed, time, and harvest may feel kind of like the proverbial tortoise racing against the hare. Just remember the tortoise won.

Sustain the Sizzle!

It seems like every day some "expert" comes up with the next-best-marketing-strategy-thing to make your growth explode. This can make you feel like you are drowning in new stuff while still trying to figure out the old stuff - which might only be a few weeks or months old, but the "gurus of the new" make it seem like what was said previously is all of a sudden ancient history. I have come to the realization that if you try to do everything that every expert tells you to do with your marketing, it will lead to frustration, futility and eventually failure.

Many entrepreneurs go looking for the "big bang" approach to marketing. However, because our society has such a short attention span, even if they liked what you did today, they will have forgotten about you next week because of the next best thing that now has their attention. That is how you become a short-lived novelty, not how you build long-term brand loyalty.

Marketing is really about have a multi-pronged approach to establishing your brand in the minds and hearts of people (just because you get in their heads doesn't automatically mean you have their hearts). It is multiple pieces on multiple levels with multiple applications that you have to implement over time.

Patience is the key. Without it you may just be another flash in the pan that was here today and gone tomorrow.

《《❖》》

B.I.G. Idea:
If God ordained it He will sustain it!

《《❖》》

Marketing Action Plan

Many Christians assume because God has called them into business they can just "show up" in the marketplace and He is going to automatically bless what they do. His promises are only guaranteed to come true for you when you follow His instructions. Unfortunately, one key area where many Christian business owners invite failure is in marketing, because they don't do their research, create a comprehensive strategic marketing plan, or execute it with diligence and excellence.

Your promise land is currently occupied by giants who must be dispossessed before you can possess it fully. You must understand who they are and evaluate their strengths and weaknesses so you can defeat them decisively. Whether we are talking about spiritual enemies or business competitors, never underestimate your opposition. God has already given you the victory, but you must rely on Him for the business ideas, concepts and strategies that will position you to occupy your promise land. This process of trusting God is developing discipline and preparing you for bigger giants and greater victories down the line.

The purpose of a marketing action plan is to develop a comprehensive strategy for communicating your value to current and potential customers. The foundation of an effective marketing plan is quality research.

Key Questions: Your customer is not "everybody," it's not "anybody," it's specifically "somebody." So, just like a reporter you need to ask some probing questions about your target audience which will give you the necessary information to build a comprehensive profile of your ideal customer. Once you thoroughly understand what their characteristics and tendencies are you can be much more effective in connecting with them. Here are some of the key questions you need to be asking:

- ⇨ **WHO** are your target customers?
- ⇨ **WHAT** are their key attributes and characteristics?
- ⇨ **WHEN** do they spend their money?
- ⇨ **WHERE** do they spend their money?
- ⇨ **WHY** do they spend their money in that manner?
- ⇨ **HOW** do they spend their money, i.e. freely or conservatively?

Marketing Data: There are many ways to discover the needs, issues, and desires of your target customers. Various types of data can be used to build a comprehensive profile of them.

- ✓ Demographics
- ✓ Socioeconomic conditions
- ✓ Seasonal trends
- ✓ Lifestyle patterns, trends, needs, and preferences
- ✓ Psychographics: interests, attitudes, opinions
- ✓ Behavior: usage rate, loyalty
- ✓ Geographic
- ✓ Other

Marketing Sources: This research information can be obtained from free and paid sources.

- ✓ Customer surveys
- ✓ Competitors (market intelligence)
- ✓ Census Bureau
- ✓ Internet - web sites, news sites, blogs
- ✓ Market research companies
- ✓ Media - TV, magazines, newspapers, trade publications, other
- ✓ Courthouse records
- ✓ Library
- ✓ Friends and neighbors
- ✓ Other

Marketing Channels[1]: Once you have a good profile of your customers, several approaches to marketing can be used to connect with them.

- ✓ **Affiliate marketing**: The use by a Web site that sells products of other Web sites, called affiliates, to help market the products.
- ✓ **Content marketing**: Subscribes to the notion that delivering information to prospects and customers drives profitable consumer action. Content marketing has benefits in terms of retaining reader attention and improving brand loyalty.
- ✓ **Database marketing**: The use of customer profiles contained in a database to market to customers.
- ✓ **Direct marketing**: Utilize leaflets, brochures, letters, catalogs, or print ads mailed or distributed directly to current and potential consumers.

---

[1] Sources: www.motto.com; www.adoofa.com; www.anduro.com; www.intensedevelopment.net

✓ **Internet marketing**: Online advertising is done exclusively on the web or through the use of email. This also can include social networking web sites and tools.

✓ **Network Marketing**: A business in which a distributor network - a structured team of people - is needed to build the business by promoting and selling your products.

✓ **Permission (Email) marketing:** Marketing centered on obtaining customer consent to receive information from a company usually through email.

✓ **Referral Marketing**: The use of rewards given to current customers to promote your products and recruit other potential customers.

✓ **Search engine marketing**: The act of marketing a website via search engines, whether this be improving rank in organic listings, purchasing paid listings or a combination of these and other search engine-related activities.

✓ **Social media marketing**: Social media marketing programs usually center on efforts to create content that attracts attention and encourages readers to share it with their social networks.

Don't be overwhelmed with all the different marketing options that are available to you. Choose the platforms that will best connect your business with your current and potential customers.

5 Keys to Effective Research
1. **Dig deep**: Everything will not be obvious. Some interpretation of the data may be needed.
2. **Find experts**: Don't settle on the first source only. Identify 2 or 3 sources that confirm the same trends.
3. **Segment your time**: Spend separate time researching data versus analyzing it.
4. **Look for trends**: See what key pieces of information are interrelated/correlated. How does one impact the other?
5. **Remember your SWOT**: Especially look for information that relates to the items you pinpointed as high priorities in your SWOT. Also, check to see if something you slotted as a low priority should be higher based on the information that you find.

Seed It To See It
When you are considering using a seed-time-harvest marketing approach you have to think of yourself as a business farmer who plants lots of marketing seeds in one season with the expectation to reap the harvest in the next or a future season. With this mindset, it is important to recognize

when it is best to plant certain kinds of seeds versus others. This requires patience, timing, attention to detail, expert knowledge of your materials, and an understanding of the most beneficial planting conditions.

One of the great benefits of this strategy is that farmers get an exponential return on the seeds they plant. For every seed planted, there are many times more crops that are harvested.

The key is to use as many of these tools as possible, while getting them to work together. It is like you are building a digital tapestry that has many contact points draped across the Internet. This positions you to increase your visibility with current and potential customers, which of course enables you to find new opportunities to maximize your profitability.

If you are overwhelmed by all this, that is very understandable. Remember that you have to choose the best tools that are going to work for you within a comprehensive strategy, system and process. Without these, you will become overwhelmed, frustrated and ineffective.

Kingdom entrepreneurs have an incredible competitive advantage when they use the Word of God and the Holy Spirit to guide their business endeavors. So don't overlook or underestimate key principles found in the Bible that should be applied to your marketing game plan. These principles can result in great influence and prosperity.

《《❖》》

B.I.G. Idea:
Kingdom building entrepreneurs have the best competitive advantage when they use the Word of God and the Holy Spirit to guide their business endeavors.

《《❖》》

Exercise: Develop a customer profile for your target customers. Answer the marketing action plan key questions (who, what where, etc.) by doing the following:

1) Identify relevant data needed for your business and customer.
2) Identify three to five marketing resources.
3) Utilize 8 to 10 key pieces of information from your market research.
4) Analyze data to identify customer trends.

Customer Profile

⇨ **WHO** are your target customers?

⇨ **WHAT** are their key attributes and characteristics?

⇨ **WHEN** do they spend their money?

⇨ **WHERE** do they spend their money?

⇨ **WHY** do they spend their money in that manner?

⇨ **HOW** do they spend their money, i.e. freely or conservatively?

Exercise 2: Identify your business revenue model and the specific products and services you will offer to your key customers.

Exercise 3: Create a practice strategy map for your Product/Service.
1) Incorporate market research information.
2) Address short, medium, and long-term priorities that you identified in your SWOT ratings.
3) Marketing strategy map should support and align with company growth goals.

Marketing Strategy Map

<u>Goals</u>   <u>Objectives</u>   <u>Initiatives</u>   <u>Actions</u>

SECTION III

DO IT!

CHAPTER 12

MY ACTION PLANS

"A slack hand causes poverty,
but the hand of the diligent makes rich."
Proverbs 10:4

V-STAR BUSINESS PLANNING SYSTEM

**Vision, Mission,
& Values**
What & Why?

Results
Measures?

**C.O.R.E.
Focus**

Strategy
How?

Action Planning
What & When?

Target Market
Who?

Multiplication Miracles Happen in Your Hands

When it comes to dealing with money, it often seems like many Christians want God to make things happen for them and bring them the results, all without much of their involvement. For some it's easy to "name it and claim it" (or as some would say, "blab it and grab it"), and then wait around for an angel to whisk a special delivery blessing on a chariot to their doorstep, like they were receiving a package from a heavenly UPS delivery person.

It's interesting, though, throughout Scripture we very rarely see God providing money as a means of deliverance or breakthrough. However, we do witness a pattern of God's expectation of our participation in His plans. This method started in the Garden of Eden with God providing for Adam's needs as he fulfilled his task of nurturing the agriculture and naming the animals. It continues as a theme throughout the Bible, especially with the demonstration of miracles. With the Old Testament prophets, Jesus, and the Apostles we usually see people actively participating in their own deliverance, not just merely receiving a blessing.

God has always desired to work in partnership with us. He does not want us just sitting idly while watching Him work, nor does He just want to watch us work without His involvement. One expression of God's desire for intimate fellowship is through the opportunity to engage Him as we are operating in the area of our purpose.

A great example of this is the account of the feeding of the five thousand referenced in John 6:1-14. A young boy and the disciples each played a key role in the miracle that greatly impacted what many Biblical scholars say was the largest crowd that Jesus gathered at any one time (the number fed was probably between 15,000 to 20,000 because the scripture references 5000 *men*, which does not include the women and children which were most likely present). So what can we learn from the active participants in this miracle that you can apply to your business?

1) **Jesus**: He will challenge us to engage with him in blessing others. Jesus easily could have performed this miracle without the disciples help. However, he wanted them to see how important they were in God's plans. You and your business can be a vital part of what He is doing in the earth if you are willing to submit you and it to him.

2) **Young boy**: He gave what he had. Jesus used what was already in that little lad's hands. We can only bring to Jesus what we have even if we do not consider it as something great. Jesus will easily take something small and make it great.

3) **Disciples**: Although they were reluctant at first, mainly because they didn't have enough money to buy food for everyone, the disciples obeyed Jesus' command to go find some food. And even though they did not think much of what they had found it was just enough for

Jesus to do something spectacular with it. Your belief and obedience is required to see miracles happen in and through your business.

One of the most significant revelations drawn from this account is the fact that the fish and five loaves did not begin to multiply until the disciples started giving away what Jesus had blessed (Mark 6:41). The miracle didn't manifest until they participated in the process with Jesus. Likewise, amazing moments like these will not occur in your life until you decide to participate with God in His plans to transform your family, community, business, industry, etc. He will bless your talents, gifts, resources, and anything else that you offer to Him. But then it's up to you to use what He blesses to bless others. Then you will see miracles of multiplication.

* * * * *

"Therefore, prepare your minds for action..."
1 Peter 1:13

* * * * *

Close the Gap

One main reason why we do not see more profitable Kingdom entrepreneurs and enterprises is because of the gap that exists between knowing what to do and doing what you know. I call this the "success gap." The wider the distance between knowing and doing, the greater commitment you must make to do the work it is going to take to get to where you should be. You have to get good at implementing what you learn in order for it to profit you and your business.

That is the main reason I wrote this book in the form of an interactive workbook. I wanted to make it easy for you to make the transition from learning to doing.

Some Christians do not understand or value the spiritual connection to planning. Yet even God values the importance of planning. In Jeremiah 29:11 He says to us, *"For I know the plans I have for you, declares the LORD, plans for welfare and not for evil, to give you a future and a hope."*

Just remember, a mediocre plan executed well is better than a great plan executed poorly.

〈〈〈❖〉〉〉

B.I.G. Idea:
A mediocre plan executed well is better than a great plan executed poorly.

〈〈〈❖〉〉〉

Lights! Camera! Action!

This is where this gets really real. This is where you truly find out if you are ready to commit to this entrepreneurial journey. Now it's time to implement your idea by executing your plan.

When it comes to action planning, few words are needed. It's time to implement what you have been preparing with your strategy maps. Just like the strategy maps, you need to develop action plans for each of your five core business functions:

1) **People**: Team building, partnership development.
2) **Products & Services**: Product development, marketing.
3) **Processes**: Company infrastructure, efficient best practices.
4) **Performance Management**: Evaluation and improvement.
5) **Profit Management**: Financial management.

Here are the key questions you need to ask yourself for each of these functions. The more precise you can be with your answers, the more confident you will be that you are moving in the right direction. As you contemplate the answers to these questions, insert your answers in the planning worksheets at the end of this chapter.

1) What steps need to be implemented to execute your strategy? What critical actions need to take place for you to move forward?
2) Who will be your team to provide coaching, support, accountability, and resources? Find 3 to 5 quality people with complementary vision and skills who want to build with you. If finances are initially an issue, barter with experts for essential services that you need to move your business forward.
3) Where are you going to do it? Define where your activities will take place. Be very specific, whether it's online or offline.
4) How will you do it (in-person, phone, email, internet, etc.)? Select the best tools that will be the most appropriate for the activities that you choose.
5) When are you going to execute? What is your Phase 1, 2, or 3? Give yourself deadlines and stick to them. Share your deadlines with someone on your team, so they can help to hold you accountable.

Financial Planning and Fundraising Strategies

Prior to any business launch you must calculate your startup costs and gather your financial resources, especially cash that is easy to access. Cash is like the blood of a business and cash flow is its circulatory system. And just like the human body sometimes needs a blood transfusion, businesses often need cash infusions to launch, maintain, and sustain their operations.

Any business that is going to succeed and become sustainable must become profitable, where those profits can be used to invest back into the business for expansion purposes. However, profitability can often take a long time to materialize and many businesses need financial infusions long before they become profitable. Fortunately for businesses that need immediate capital, several solutions exist that can provide a financial boost to companies. Here are a few of them (Source: Investopedia, www.investopedia.com):

1) **Asset-Based Financing:** A specialized method of providing structured working capital and term loans that are secured by accounts receivable, inventory, machinery, equipment and/or real estate.

2) **Angel Investing:** Angel investors give more favorable terms than other lenders, as they are usually investing in the person rather than the viability of the business. They are focused on helping the business succeed, rather than reaping a huge profit from their investment. Angel investors are essentially the exact opposite of a venture capitalist.

3) **Crowd Funding:** Internet based, campaign-style fundraising platform that leverages the power and functionality of social media marketing. Funds are usually raised from friends, friends of friends, and others who believe in your business model are have desire to see it succeed. However, unlike traditional venture capital, you can receive funds without having to give up shares of ownership to donors.

4) **Factoring:** The sale of accounts receivables is called factoring. Factoring companies will purchase your receivables for a percentage fee.

5) **Microcredit:** The extension of very small loans (microloans) to borrowers who typically lack the business history, collateral, and/or verifiable credit history that traditional banks use to secure loans.

6) **Personal Venture Capital:** Selling shares of your company to family and friends in exchange for a certain percentage of the company's profits or a future lump sum payout with a specified date and amount of interest.

7) **Professional Venture Capital:** Money provided by investors to startup firms and small businesses with perceived long-term growth potential. Venture capital can also include managerial and technical expertise. Most venture capital comes from a group of wealthy investors, investment banks and other financial institutions that pool such investments or partnerships.

There are pros and cons for each of these funding options. I suggest you do further research on each to determine which one(s) is right for your business.

Action Planning Tools
Checklists
A checklist is a set of directions or instructions that ensure all essential activities or assignments are completed in a process. "Un-complicate" your process and transfer your knowledge to paper and other people.

Checklist Tips
✓ **Documentation**: Write down the specific activities/steps and keep the document in an accessible location.
✓ **Designee**: Identify the person responsible for the completion of the process.
✓ **Directions**: Clearly write all steps that need to be completed.
✓ **Details**: Be specific so that the steps/activities can be easily understood.
✓ **Deadlines**: State the required time frame all the activities are to be completed.
✓ **Diagrams**: Utilize pictures to assist with clarity.

Flowcharts
A flowchart is a step-by-step, visual description of a single process. They are excellent tools to understand all the moving parts of an individual process and the interdependencies of multiple processes. They help you replicate successful processes. Additionally, they allow you to identify specific steps in a process that might be causing continual disruptions, problems, issues, or inefficiencies that create barriers or delays to providing value to your customers.

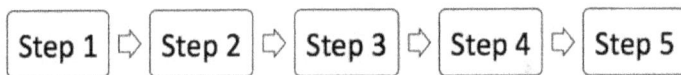

| Step 1 | ⇨ | Step 2 | ⇨ | Step 3 | ⇨ | Step 4 | ⇨ | Step 5 |

I suggest that you use flip charts that you can post onto a wall in your work area and leave them there so that you have a constant reminder of where you are in your implementation process and timeline.

Planning Worksheets

Note: You may want to recreate these tables in a spreadsheet, which would be easier to facilitate.

1) PEOPLE	PHASE 1	PHASE 2	PHASE 3
What?			
Who?			
Where?			
How?			
When?			

2) PRODUCTS & SERVICES	PHASE 1	PHASE 2	PHASE 3
What?			
Who?			
Where?			
How?			
When?			

3) PROCESSES	PHASE 1	PHASE 2	PHASE 3
What?			
Who?			
Where?			
How?			
When?			

4) PERFORMANCE MANAGEMENT	PHASE 1	PHASE 2	PHASE 3
What?			
Who?			
Where?			
How?			
When?			

5) PROFIT MANAGEMENT	PHASE 1	PHASE 2	PHASE 3
What?			
Who?			
Where?			
How?			
When?			

CHAPTER 13

MAXIMIZE MY MANAGMENT

"Know well the condition of your flocks, and give attention to your herds."
Proverbs 27:23

V-STAR BUSINESS PLANNING SYSTEM

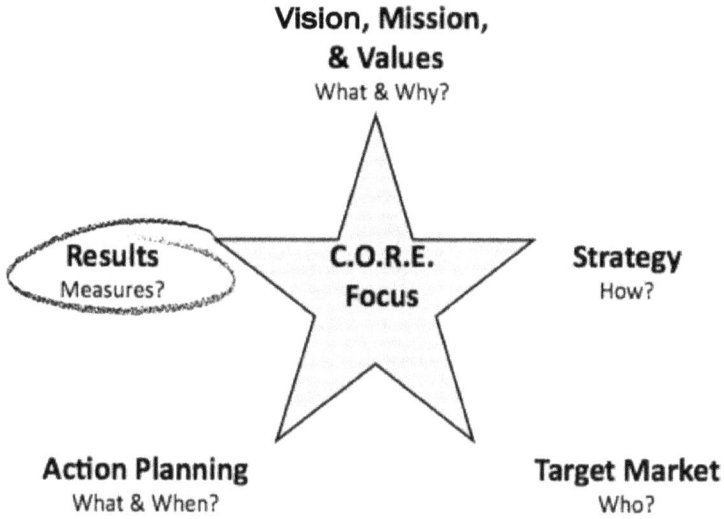

**Vision, Mission,
& Values**
What & Why?

Results
Measures?

**C.O.R.E.
Focus**

Strategy
How?

Action Planning
What & When?

Target Market
Who?

How Would Jesus Lead Your Company?

Although we can look around our society and see many great examples of effective business leaders, the one person that will always be the gold standard is Jesus. Remember, he had a compelling vision, launched a successful startup franchise, was an excellent communicator, had a unique life-changing solution that produced amazing results, recruited and trained a high performance team, specialized in his niche market, dominated his competitors, his customers became raving fans and his most successful marketers, and he implemented a leadership succession plan that has resulted in his business continuing to grow exponentially for more than 2000 years. We continue to glean so much wisdom and so many practical applications from his model that people are still writing books about his life and business today.

So why don't we see more Christian CEOs who have been able to replicate his success? After all he did say we would do greater works than he did (John 14:12). Could it be that although we yield to him in other areas of our lives we are not following in his business leadership and management footsteps?

In the world of Christian entrepreneurship it often seems like there is a huge supply of ideas but a lack of wisdom, as in implementation and execution with fruitfulness. I write this on the basis of observing a lot of Christian entrepreneurs who rely on trial and error without a lot of surety when it comes to implementing what they say they heard from God. However, the word of God tells us in James 1 that He gives wisdom liberally to those who ask for it.

Jesus was always in the right place at the right time doing the right things, primarily because he spent so much time with God. He taught us that he *only* did the works of his Father (John 10:37) and what his Father showed him (John 5:19).

Maybe if Christian entrepreneurs spent more time on our faces versus on Facebook we would receive more direct revelation from God that would be applicable to our businesses. I am not bashing social media (I use it a lot), but what I am saying is that if everyday we are only waiting on social media or TV or the Internet or any other source rather than God for instruction and direction then we will continue on the path of trial and error, resulting in us taking longer to get to the promise land where God has already prepared for us and our businesses to succeed. Now of course God can use any source to download wisdom to us, however His primary desire is that we will connect with Him more one-to-one.

Proportional accuracy is the correlation between how much time we spend with God and how accurate we are in our decision-making. This is not a measure of a specific ratio or any other type of mathematical formula, but is more of a spiritual indicator that is applied through self-evaluation to understand and recognize the opportunity to get more things right and fewer things wrong. If Jesus was truly leading your business as the CEO he would be more than proportionally accurate. He would be 100% accurate all the time.

The very first question he would likely ask is, *"Am I doing what God said to do to make this business profitable and sustainable or am I following the crowd, doing whatever everyone else has said to do to be successful?"* I'm sure he would ask a lot more questions – Scripture shows us that Jesus liked questions – but this is a good start to help you determine if you are headed in the right direction and functioning optimally. The rest of the questions and answers will come as you spend more quality time with Him.

⟨⟨⟨❖⟩⟩⟩

B.I.G. Idea:
How would Jesus lead your business differently than you?

⟨⟨⟨❖⟩⟩⟩

God Inspired Operations Management

V-STAR is a God inspired business leadership and performance management system that draws from His wisdom with the intent of providing a comprehensive and practical way to launch, lead, and grow your business. He formed the idea in my mind over a number of years drawing from my diverse experiences at work, consulting engagements, undergraduate and graduate business school education, leadership positions at a large church, and my personal Bible studies.

My hope is that as you have been going through this process you would recognize that V-STAR has the capacity and potential to become the operations management DNA of your business. Not only can it be used as the overall management philosophy/structure of your company, you can use the model to manage each of the five core business functions defined in this book.

* * * * *

"If you aim at nothing, you will hit it every time."
~Zig Ziglar

* * * * *

The final component of this model, which will be discussed in this chapter, is one of the most important aspects. This particular activity,

Results Management, provides the practical indicators for you to know how successful you are in achieving your vision, implementing your strategy, reaching your target market, and executing your action plan.

An effective principle initiated by God, and now used in the business world is you must "inspect what you expect" (1 Samuel 16:7, Psalm 9:8, Matthew 7:20, Hebrews 4:12). This simply means that whatever outcome you say that you desire, you must have a means of evaluating and determining whether you are getting closer to or further away from that goal. Results Management provides a set of tools that allow you to do this effectively with your business.

Measure, Monitor, and Make Adjustments

Throughout this book I have discussed the importance of Kingdom CEOs measuring your progress by a more comprehensive holistic standard than other entrepreneurs use. In particular, the Triple Bottom Line approach allows you to assess your business through a godly lens as you evaluate the financial, spiritual, and social health of your operations.

Just like with your physical body, if you never take the time to assess the health of your business you will not realize or ignore the indicators that let you know when you are in distress. And just like your doctor would provide tests and tools to help you recognize key aspects of your physical health, the following performance management tools and techniques in order to effectively execute your business strategy using objective criteria. These three activities assist you with the process and information needed to grow what we have defined as a healthy and sustainable Kingdom business.

Triple Bottom Line

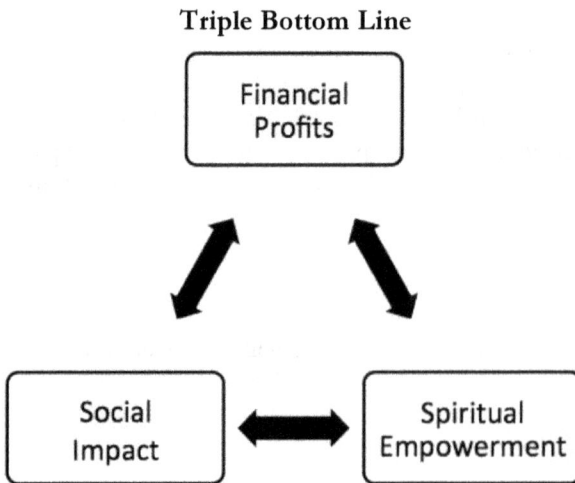

1) **Monitor**: Reviewing your results on a regular basis to determine the health of your business.
2) **Measure**: Specific key performance indicators (KPIs) that reveal what is happening within your business operations.
3) **Make adjustments**: The steps you take to redirect negative performance or accelerate positive performance.

Why Performance Metrics Matter

Similar to a dashboard on a car, performance metrics can be used internally to help gauge how well your processes are performing. They can be used externally to help you confirm or validate the effectiveness of your products with your customers, which will help your business establish strategic market positioning. Some companies do not know they are in trouble until they are in trouble.

* * * * *

"An ounce of prevention is better than a pound of cure."
~Benjamin Franklin

* * * * *

You might be thinking that performance management metrics are something only big companies need. However, small businesses can get many benefits from having a solid performance management metrics in place, including:
1) Metrics are a dashboard for your goals.
2) Metrics bring focus to things that matter.
3) What gets measured gets focus.
4) Metrics can be used to motivate your team.
5) Continually raise the bar with stretch goals.
6) Baseline information for performance improvement.

Key Performance Indicators

Performance measurement precedes performance management. You cannot effectively manage or make improvements to something you have not measured. Key Performance Indicators (KPI) are metrics that quantify how well (or not) your business is functioning in different areas. Using these metrics allows you to be able to gauge the health of your company with quantifiable data from your operations (see table on the next page).

Performance measurement and management is an on-going activity, not just a one-time event. You won't get the full effect if you do it haphazardly or randomly. You must incorporate it into your operational processes. I will describe some very practical ways that you can effectively monitor, measure, and make adjustments to your business performance based on the results that you experience.

* * * * *

"Discipline is the bridge between goals and accomplishment."
~Jim Rohn

* * * * *

Continuous Performance Improvement

Continuous performance improvement is a process not just a random activity. It is extremely important that you put a plan and process around your efforts to continuously improve your performance, because that will allow you to understand the impact of the changes you make. Then you can duplicate what is successful and discontinue what does not work.

Continuous performance improvement begins with an attitude that must be embraced by you and everyone associated with your company. Everyone must feel that part of their job is to improve how your business develops and delivers its products/services, supports customers, takes advantage of opportunities, manages results, stewards money, and impacts the community.

The following steps will walk you through a continuous performance improvement process using the three activities that I alluded to earlier in this chapter:

1) **Monitor**
   - ✓ Identify key performance indicators (KPI) within the five core business functions that are relevant to your business success and sustainability.
   - ✓ Review KPIs on a consistent schedule (daily, weekly, monthly, etc.)

2) **Measure**
   - ✓ Identify trouble areas in your business that give you constant headaches.
   - ✓ Measure current performance gaps against your KPIs.
   - ✓ Establish baseline performance data.
   - ✓ Identify key internal issues and reasons for performance gaps.
   - ✓ Try to distinguish if what you are seeing is static historic data versus an indication of future trends.

3) **Make adjustments**
   - ✓ Develop and implement action plans to close specific, critical performance gaps.

- ✓ Determine corrective actions that are needed to close gaps and improve performance.
- ✓ Redesign processes or procedures as needed.
- ✓ Implement new processes and procedures as needed.
- ✓ Insert changes into goals statement and strategy maps.
- ✓ Monitor and measure new operational processes for progress.

Sample Key Performance Indicators

Core Function	KPIs Examples	Why it's important to your business
People	1) Employee satisfaction 2) Employee productivity 3) Employee retention	
Products & Services	1) Sales 2) Revenues 3) Customer acquisition rate 4) Customer satisfaction rating 5) Customer retention 6) Sales cycle time 7) Returns/cancellations 8) Reliability (low defects)	
Processes	1) Time to market 2) Operational efficiency 3) Productivity 4) Quality (product defects) 5) Sales cycle time	
Performance Management	1) Progress toward company goals 2) Operational efficiency 3) Sales cycle time	
Profit Management	2) Sales 3) Revenues 4) Profits 5) Revenue per customer 6) Revenue per product/service 7) Operational costs 8) Financial ratios	

After you have monitored and measured your performance you must be committed to making adjustments that make sense. If you are not willing to make adjustments to how you lead and manage your business you are wasting your time monitoring and measuring your performance.

Continuous Improvement Recommendation

Core Function	Continuous Performance Improvement Recommendations
People	✓ Focus on personal growth and professional development activities. ✓ Integrate continuous learning and teaching into core business practices. ✓ Create/change new roles and responsibilities as needed. ✓ Establish and implement succession plans.
Products & Services	✓ Continuously exceed customer expectations. ✓ Stay ahead of the curve in terms of meeting customer's needs. ✓ Adjust pricing and offerings based as needed based on your research. ✓ Enhance products/services with value-adds.
Processes	✓ Develop an on-going assessment process. ✓ Continue to raise the bar with your goals as you achieve them. ✓ Increase expertise in core competencies. ✓ Update/improve processes as experience and knowledge increases.
Performance Management	✓ Enhance and utilize core competencies. ✓ "Creative destruction": find things that need to be broken because of the status quo and fix them. ✓ Proactively develop solutions to customer problems. ✓ Look for new opportunities/niches to take advantage of core competencies.
Profit Management	✓ Stakeholder value continuously increases. ✓ ROI should continue to meet or exceed goals. ✓ Stakeholders benefit directly from the performance of the organization. ✓ Use cash flow for internal reinvestment and equipment upgrades.

As you identify KPIs for your five core business functions, you must determine how monitoring, measuring, and making adjustments is going to directly or indirectly impact your bottom line(s). Otherwise, this will become just disconnected information that has no relevant impact on your business. That is why now we are going to look at how to utilize performance management metrics that are directly focused on the three components of the Triple Bottom Line.

Customer Relationship Management

How would Jesus serve your customers? I wrote earlier about the critical importance to your business of loving your customers by serving them well. Jesus clearly demonstrated to us that he came to serve and not be served. Likewise, the focus of your business should be serving your customers with excellence.

Nevertheless, I understand that sometimes it may be hard to wrap your mind around this concept if you have never considered the implications or practical applications of serving your customers. Fortunately, we have some guidelines in the Word of God that can help you to understand what loving your customer looks like.

In 1 Corinthians 13:4-6, I count fifteen different character qualities that love represents that you can use to guide how you interact with your customers. They include:

1) Love is patient.
2) Love is kind.
3) Love is not jealous.
4) Love is not boastful.
5) Love is not proud.
6) Love is not rude.
7) Love doesn't demand its own way.
8) Love is not irritable.
9) Love doesn't keep a record of being wronged.
10) Love doesn't rejoice about injustice.
11) Love rejoices when the truth wins out.
12) Love never gives up.
13) Love never loses faith.
14) Love is always hopeful.
15) Love endures through every circumstance.

Similarly to how I encouraged you to incorporate the "Fruit of the Spirit" in your company values, it would be a great idea to incorporate these love principles into your customer service policies and customer relationship management practices. You may not include every one of these characteristics individually, however, you can incorporate the ones that make sense and are easy to measure quantitatively or qualitatively. You will be surprised by the blessings and benefits you will receive by intentionally incorporating God Word and His principles into your daily business activities.

《《《❖》》》

B.I.G. Idea:
How well you love people through your business will be a
major factor in your overall profitability.

《《《❖》》》

These days there is a lost appreciation for great customer service for the sake of saving a few dollars. However, you can buck this trend and stand out from your competitors if you are willing to implement some best practices that I refer to as the Great 8's of Customer Relationship Management:

1) **Investigate** what the best companies in the world do to create dynamic customer experiences.
2) **Evaluate** how you can apply the best practices that are most relevant and cost effective for your business.
3) **Demonstrate** a commitment to fanatical customer service by implementing relevant policies, processes, and practices.
4) **Eliminate** unnecessary things that make it harder for your customer to do business with you.
5) **Appreciate** your customers in special ways at different times throughout the year.
6) **Facilitate** surveys and other tools that will give you continuous feedback of how your customers feel about your company.
7) **Celebrate** your customer service success with your team and reward them for a job well done.
8) **Elevate** your business above your competition through a continued commitment to exemplary customer service.

Don't cut corners on how you treat your customers. After all they are necessary for you to be successful in business. Besides, it's fun to serve with a spirit of excellence and be rewarded for it!

Financial Management
Stewarding God's Money

As a marketplace priest God is entrusting you with the responsibility to steward His earthly resources. God owns everything, which means the income generated by your business is not for you primarily. He gives us the power to get wealth in order to establish His covenant in the earth. So we must continually seek His will for what He wants us to do with His money. Of course He will allow us to take care of our needs, but we cannot become consumed with our own bills and desires. The more we demonstrate that we are trustworthy the more He will entrust to our oversight for stewardship and pleasure. For some that will be billions, for others millions, and for others maybe only thousands. Regardless, handle His money with care.

The Perverted Pursuit of Profits Can Poison Your Purity

Kingdom CEOs walk a fine line because so much of what we do is directly connected to money. The reality is you can't grow a sustainable, flourishing business that honors God without continually generating healthy profits. The problem comes when financial gain replaces your first priority to seek first the Kingdom of God and His righteousness. God doesn't have a problem with you possessing things. He just doesn't want things possessing you. That's why Kingdom business leaders must stay close to God in order to maintain a pure heart toward His purposes. The pursuit of profits must be connected to His purposes not your own plans.

The most valuable asset you possess is your reputation, so it is absolutely necessary that you operate in the marketplace with absolute integrity. Furthermore, you're representing Christ which means that you're working for him not yourself. Real trust in God means you don't have to manipulate people to get what you want. When you honor God with your honesty, He will honor you with His blessings.

Managing Expenses

In the earlier chapter focused on pricing and positioning I discussed with you the need to look at increasing your revenues as a means for increasing your profitability. Well, the other side of that equation of maximizing your profitability is decreasing your expenses.

Profits = Income - Expenses

The total expenses for your business equal your fix costs plus your average variable costs multiplied times the quantity of your sales.

> ## Total Expenses =
> ## Fixed Costs +
> ## Average Variable Costs x Quantity

Strategies to decrease expenses should include:
1) Lower fixed costs: rent, insurance, taxes, utilities, etc.
2) Lower variable costs: direct labor, inventory, raw materials
3) Increase efficiency: streamlined processes and using fewer resources (how can you do more with less?)

Break Even Analysis

How much income do you need to produce so that your income equals your expenses? Based on your sales projections, how long will it take for your income to exceed your expenses, i.e. so that you are profitable (calculated in months or years)?

Expenses		Income
Variable Costs +	**Fixed Costs** =	**Sales**
Cost of Goods Sold	Salaries	Total Income
Inventory	Advertising	(# of Customers x
Raw Materials	Equipment	Price)
Direct Labor (incl.	Utilities	
payroll taxes)	Rent	
	Taxes	
	Interest	
	Benefits	
	Other	

> ## Total Income – (Variable Costs + Fixed Costs) =
> ## $0 (Break Even)

Accounting Analysis

Analyzing your financial statements will provide greater insights to your current financial condition. These statements are "dashboard" indicators to help you determine how well your company is operating. Important financial statements that need to be reviewed include the following:

⇨ **Balance Sheet**: also referred to as statement of financial position or condition, reports on a company's assets, liabilities, and ownership equity at a given point in time.

Sample Balance Sheet

Kingdom Business, Inc. For the year ended December 31, 2013		
Revenue	$	$
GROSS Profit (including rental income)		496,397
Expenses		
Advertising	6300	
Bank & Credit Card Fees	144	
Bookkeeping	3350	
Employees	88,000	
Entertainment	5550	
Insurance	750	
Legal & Professional Services	1575	
Licenses	632	
Printing, postage, & stationery	320	
Rent	13,000	
Rental Mortgage and Fees	74,400	
Utilities	491	
Total Expenses		(194, 512)
Net Income		$301, 885

⇨ **Statement of Retained Earnings**: Explains the changes in a company's retained earnings over the reporting period.

Sample Statement of Retained Earnings

Kingdom Business, Inc. For the Year Ended Dec. 31, 2013	
Retained earnings January 1, 2013	100,000
Add: Net income for Year (from Income Statement)	301,885
Deduct: Withdrawals for the Year	50,000
Retained earnings December 31, 2013	**$351,885**

⇨ **Statement of Cash Flows**: Explains the changes in a company's cash assets over the reporting period.

Sample Statement of Cash Flows

Kingdom Business, Inc. For the Quarter Ended December 13, 2013			
	October	November	December
Start Cash Balance	$15,000	$7,177.00	$12,454.00
Cash Sales	$8,457	$17,277	$10,846
Owner Investment	$0	$0	$0
Accounts Receivable	$220	$5,000	$3,500
Other	$0	$0	$0
Total Cash in	$8,677	$22,277	$14,346
Cash Out			
Fixed Expenses	$(5,000)	$(5,000)	$(5,000)
Variable Expenses	$(11,500)	$(12,000)	$(11,300)
Total Cash Out	$(16,500)	$(17,000)	$(16,300)
Total Cash Balance	**$7,177**	**$12,454**	**$10,500**

⇨ **Financial Ratios**: Simple mathematical comparisons of two or more entries from a company's financial statements. Business owners and managers use ratios to chart a company's progress, uncover trends and point to potential problem areas in a business. Bankers and investors look at a company's ratios when they are trying to decide if they want to lend you money or invest in your company. Here are some that are commonly used and most relevant to you (Source: Bankrate.com):

Standard Financial Ratios

Ratio	Definition/Purpose
Current ratio	Measures your company's liquidity and ability to pay short-term debts by comparing current assets to current liabilities.
Quick ratio	Another liquidity ratio, commonly called the "acid test." It compares current assets, less inventory, to current liabilities to determine how readily you can convert to cash to pay current obligations.
Debt to Assets	Measures how much a company relies on borrowing to finance operations, an important ratio if you're interested in getting a loan.
Return on Investment (ROI)	Measures how well the investment in the company is performing and is calculated by dividing net profits by total assets.
Return on Assets (ROA)	Measures how much income your assets generate.
Gross Profit Margin	Measures the amount of each dollar that can go for overhead and profit.
Operating Profit Percentage	Measures the profitability of your core business.

According to information provided by Bankrate.com:
Ratios provide insight into every financial element in your company, from its profitability to the effectiveness of your accounts receivable department. We've put together calculators for some of the most commonly used business ratios.

When you compare today's ratios to last year's or a compilation of several years' records, it can help you chart your progress and plan for the future. Once compiled, you can also use ratios to compare your company's performance with others within your industry. You'll find industry comparisons in publications such as Robert Morris' Annual Statement Studies, the Almanac of Business and Industrial Financial Ratios (published by Prentiss Hall) or key business ratios, published by Dun & Bradstreet.

For additional information on financial ratios, please visit Bankrate.com. They even have calculators for each of the financial ratios mentioned above.

Additional Financial Analysis
A company often has many, sometimes less than obvious, options that will impact its profitability. Additional ways to reduce your expenses and maximize your profits:

⇨ **Product/Price Mix**: Determining which products/services to sell at which price.

⇨ **Do-It-Yourself vs. Buying it**: Choosing between something that you can purchase versus making it yourself (could relate to materials or services).

⇨ **Buy vs. Lease**: Choosing the best long-term financial benefit between these two options (usually when considering property or equipment).

⇨ **Tax reduction strategies**: Hire an excellent accountant!

As I stated earlier, it is absolutely vital that you surround yourself with some accounting and tax experts to ensure that you are managing your business well from a financial perspective. They will save you a lot of headaches and money.

A Note on Tithing
Giving money is a key way that God tests the heart of His people. He is a giver and therefore how closely we reflect the nature of God is directly correlated to our obedience in how we conduct ourselves in the area of money according to the protocols He established. The Bible is clear that individuals should tithe off the their gross income, not the net. However, it's not as clear from which Kingdom businesses should tithe. For many small businesses it would be nearly impossible to tithe off their gross income without putting themselves in financial peril due thin profit margins based on the type of business they operate. Nevertheless, this is a faith growing opportunity for Kingdom entrepreneurs.

I suggest you start tithing to your local church from your net profits and then begin to increase it over time until you can tithe from your gross income. God is faithful to abundantly bless those who give with sincerity, joy, and an expectation for a return on their investment in the Kingdom.

Spiritual Growth Management

God's goal for you is not to compartmentalize your walk with Him, as in disconnecting spiritual matters from you business operations. They are very much integrated. Therefore, your spiritual management will have a direct effect on your financial profits and vice versa.

In the earlier chapter about your vision, mission, and values, I wrote about how you can consider utilizing the Fruit of the Spirit found in Galatians 5 as a way of practically integrating the Kingdom of Heaven culture in your business (see table below). So if you are going to adhere to the theme of this chapter – inspect what you expect – you should evaluate how you well you are applying these principles in your work environment.

An easy way to do this is include specific questions related to these spiritual best practices in surveys that you would typically give to your customers, employees, suppliers, community, and other stakeholders. You do not have to label them to stand out from your other questions. The feedback you receive from these different parties will let you know how well you are operating with a Kingdom culture.

It is also possible to look at your operational and financial KPIs to determine how well you are functioning with a Kingdom culture. The key is for you to review your metrics with natural and spiritual eyes. You need to be honest with what you discover and not over-spiritualize the facts if your business is struggling in certain areas. However, it would be wise to ask the Holy Spirit for revelation beyond the raw data and performance metrics so he can help you interpret what you see and then direct you to make the proper adjustments.

Spiritually Based Business KPIs

Spiritual Best Practices	Business Best Practices	KPI Measurement
Love	Focus on serving customers and meeting needs, not making money (as a priority) Genuinely caring for customer and employees needs Selflessness displayed consistently	
Joy	Passion Excitement Contagious attitude	
Peace	Mediators of conflict Settle conflicts quickly and fairly Cooperative relationships Win-win partnerships	
Kindness	Fanatical commitment to customer service Environment to fail safely Exceed expectations Generosity	
Goodness	Proactively providing solutions that help people Business excellence Creativity and innovation Industry leader	
Faithfulness	Stay true to your brand Integrity in all dealings Moral and ethical practices Consistency of purpose	
Meekness	Servant leadership Power/influence under control Strength of character "Humbition": Humble yet bold ambitions	
Self-Control	Visionary: Always act with the end in mind Disciplined thought, action, words Streamlined, efficient operations	

Social Impact Management

Of the three components of the Triple Bottom Line, social impact can sometimes be the hardest to quantify and evaluate. However, some basic principles apply that will give you some guidance as to how to incorporate this area in the overall assessment of your company's health.

The first thing to consider is similar to the maxim taught in school to all healthcare students and is a fundamental principle throughout the world, which states, *"First, do no harm."* Your business should do no harm to people or the planet (environmental). As a good steward of what God has entrust you with, it definitely would not be good for your relationship with Him if you are using your business to harm people. That is why I would not consider you a Kingdom entrepreneur if you were engaged in any kind of business that is opposed to principles taught in God's Word. If your business could somehow drive people away from Jesus rather than closer to him, you need to pray and ask God if you need to go do something different or change how you do business.

In terms of the environmental side of this, we are not just stewards of people; we are also stewards of our planet. I am not a staunch environmentalist, but I do believe we have a responsibility to do our best to take care of what God has provided to us. You should be able to determine fairly easily whether your business is violating God's principles of taking care of the earth, especially if they have a negative impact on people's health.

I would consider "do no harm" as a passive approach to social impact management. However, I believe Kingdom entrepreneurs can be more intentional with their businesses and resources. That's what Business as Ministry is all about. In Luke 4:18-19, Jesus clearly laid out our job description as marketplace kings and priests:

> *"The Spirit of the Lord is upon me, because he has anointed me to proclaim good news to the poor. He has sent me to proclaim liberty to the captives and recovering of sight to the blind, to set at liberty those who are oppressed, to proclaim the year of the Lord's favor."*

I use the term "economic evangelism" to represent initiatives where you take the opportunity to invest your time, thoughts, talents, and treasures in bringing spiritual, economic, and social impact to struggling people and areas. Here are a few practical ways you can activate these initiatives as a Kingdom CEO:

1) **Job creation and employment**: You have an opportunity to directly affect the lives of the unemployed, underemployed, and misemployed. The bigger your company grows the more people you can employ.

2) **Vocational discipleship**: Create an environment in your business that gives people the opportunity to grow professionally and spiritually.

3) **Business development**: Help those in overlooked and forgotten communities launch and grow purpose driven businesses, which positions them to abrupt generational poverty.

4) **Economic development**: Create or invest in business development initiatives that focus on promoting godly prosperity in communities rather than ones that just talk about alleviating poverty.

5) **Community development**: Collaborate with other organizations to work on projects that improve the living conditions of disenfranchised and oppressed people.

6) **Community chaplaincy**: Provide a spiritual covering by investing your time as a friend, neighbor, or mentor in economically challenged communities.

7) **Advocacy**: Protest against systems, policies, and structures that serve to keep disenfranchised people disenfranchised.

Social impact initiatives may often take a long time to reveal the results of the activities in which you choose to engage. Nevertheless, our job is to obey God and He is responsible for the results (1 Corinthians 3:6-8). If you genuinely give your best in one or more of these areas you can be confident that He will bless your efforts. Although you may not see all the results of your investments, you will be able to experience the promise of Isaiah 58.

It is far time for us tear down the kingdom of darkness and raise up the Kingdom of Light within impoverished communities. As a Kingdom CEO you are in a prime position to do so.

Exercise 1: Define your company's key performance metrics and start capturing baseline data.
1) Determine the impact to company goals.
2) Utilize industry benchmarks.
3) Focus on using consistent measurement cycles, i.e. daily, weekly, and monthly.

Core Function	KPI Measurement	Why is it important?
People		
Products & Services		
Processes		
Performance Management		
Profit Management		

Exercise 2: Develop a Performance Management Strategy Map that will help you develop a regularly schedule time to monitor, measure, and make adjustments to your performance.
1) Review findings from your SWOT.
2) Focus on critical, high impact areas.
3) Focus on key processes.
4) Focus on only a few metrics.

Exercise 3: Spend some additional time focusing on your Spiritual Growth Management and Social Impact Management activities.
1) How can you be more intentional about creating an environment that helps to strengthen people spiritually?
2) What can you do to ensure that your business has a great impact in your community?

CHAPTER 14

THE POWER TO BECOME!

"But as many as received him, to them gave he power to become the sons
of God, even to them that believe on his name."
John 1:12

The Word Becoming Flesh

We started near the beginning of this book talking about your identity. This also how we're going to end it. The reason is you must be able to reaffirm who you are beyond what you do in order to flow with the natural highs and lows of your life and business over the long-term. This is crucial to His goal for all of His children to reflect, represent, and reproduce the image and character of Christ in all that we do.

God created you for a specific reason for a specific season. And after He created you He called you into service for His Kingdom. The beauty of this process is that God doesn't call those who are already qualified. Instead He qualifies those He calls. And part of the qualifying process is giving you the power to become just like Jesus.

You becoming an authentic representation of His Son is critical to God's plan to return back to us the earthly dominion, power, and authority that was lost by Adam. Through the work of grace by Christ on the cross, we have the incredible opportunity to embody the life of Jesus and do greater works than he did while he walked the planet. In fact all of creation is groaning in anticipation, fervently waiting for Believers to wake up to our true identity in Christ and live the powerful life that God planned for us (Romans 8:19-22). Nonetheless, you cannot reach the fullness of your potential impact in this world until you deeply embrace and incorporate the character, mindset, and essence of Jesus into your life.

⟨⟨⟨❖⟩⟩⟩

B.I.G. Idea:
Give God permission to enlarge His territory in your heart and
He will enlarge your territory in the world.

⟨⟨⟨❖⟩⟩⟩

Identity Theft

Did you know that identity theft is one of the fastest – if not the fastest – growing crimes in the United States? Over 15 million people a year experience the theft of their credit cards, bank accounts, medical information, tax refunds, utilities, and more, resulting in more than $50 billion in losses. On a case-by-case basis, approximately 1 out of every 7 adults have their identities misused with each instance resulting in approximately $3,500 in losses.

Unfortunately this issue seems to be getting worse the more that our personal information is digitized and easily accessed online. However, that is not the type of identity theft that impacts most entrepreneurs. There's another type of identity theft that happens to them everyday as they pursue ventures and opportunities in the marketplace that were not meant for them.

I have come to realize that many entrepreneurs suffer from a bad case of "mistaken identity." They have aligned their personal identity so closely with their professional image that they allow their profession to become the essence of their existence. When an entrepreneur has this syndrome, they spend most of their time focusing outside-in versus inside-out. This means they become more concerned by what they do in business than who they are as a person. They put more emphasis on their external image rather than their internal identity. These entrepreneurs place most emphasis on inventorying their businesses than they do inventorying their personal lives. It's sad to say, but they have little sense of who they are outside of their daily business activities.

One of the dangers for those individuals who have placed their entire identity solely in their profession is that if something causes a sudden or dramatic change in their business condition or professional status, a severe emotional upheaval often follows. We have all heard of those individuals who have done radical and even violent things to themselves or others as a result of bankruptcy, job loss, or other financial calamities.

《《❖》》

B.I.G. Idea:
Change will either come by revelation or tribulation.
Either way you must choose how you will respond.

《《❖》》

Change can be traumatic for anyone. However, it's even worse for those whose identity is so closely tied to the things that are changing. The reality is that you don't stop "being" just because your situation changes. Who you are stays constant. The key is knowing who you are prior to change coming. And since you can't predict when the change is coming, you must commit to a continual process of discovering and reaffirming who you are.

The truth is your value to your family, community, and society is worth so much more than what you do in your business. Your real value is in who God created you to be. Therefore, what you do as an entrepreneur should flow out of an understanding and appreciation of your life purpose and mission.

So, even when your business or profession experiences challenges that force change on you, your clear recognition of why you are alive will help guide you confidently to your next opportunity. You may not like changing and changing may be inconvenient; however, you will be able to adjust more quickly and prepare for the next opportunity that's coming to you. Your business may change, but your identity stays the same.

Becoming Like Christ in Business

Entrepreneurs are often told that in order to grow their businesses, they need to spend more time working "on" their business versus working "in" their business. I agree with this, but a more important piece of advice is often overlooked or undervalued. That advice is entrepreneurs need to spend more time working "on" themselves. If an entrepreneur spends quality time developing their character, discipline, thoughts life, and positive habits, they will be that much more effective working on and in their business.

* * * * *

"What you get by achieving your goals is not nearly as important as what you become by achieving them."
~Zig Ziglar

* * * * *

While we are all a work in progress, there are certain things we can do to be more intentional about our growth and development. Becoming a Christ-like entrepreneur is a process that requires the faithful application of specific principles. Here are three that you must incorporate into your daily life if you are to become the Christ-like entrepreneur God wants you to be:

1) **What You BELIEVE is Who You BECOME**. Your belief system is tied directly to who you are and the potential of who you can become. In 2 Corinthians 10:5, Paul tells us that we must cast down every thought and imagination that takes a higher priority over what God has said about us. He then expounds on that truth in Philippians 4:8 as he encourages us to us to focus our thoughts on things that are honest, just, good, excellent, and praiseworthy. Your belief system must be rooted in the Word of God in order to produce the life and business of your dreams.

2) **Your BELIEFS Drive Your BEHAVIOR**. Your actions are a true indication of what you really believe. Therefore, you must control the conversations that go on between your ears. You have to learn to tell your mind what to think so that what you produce with your actions is continually drawing you closer to God and your goals. If you see that your actions are drawing you away from God and your goals, the

first place of inspection is the source of what you believe. And if it's anything other than God's Word you must change the source of your belief system.

3) **Your WORDS WIN the WAR (Spiritual Warfare)**. You need to recognize that the battles we face as Believers and Kingdom entrepreneurs are primarily spiritual that result in natural consequences. Your words will either support or sabotage your faith. So one of the critical strategies of winning the spiritual war is through the words you speak in prayer and during our daily activities. You will overcome our enemies and obstacles by the words you speak in agreement with what God has already declared (Revelations 12:11). As a Kingdom leader what you decree is established in heaven and on the earth (Job 22:28, Matthew 18:18). Instead of complaining about the conditions of things that you see and don't like, you have the power to speak into existence what you want to see (Romans 4:17). Declare your victory over every situation and circumstance that doesn't line up with God's promises. The power of life and death is in your own tongue; so don't conspire with the enemy to participate your own demise.

Remember your faith is always at work building something in your life. The question is are you building something great for God or something negative based on a corrupted belief system?

* * * * *

"Doubt kills more dreams than failure ever will."
~Sandi Krakowski

* * * * *

I AM Declarations

Listed below are thirty-one declarations based on who God says you are. You can say one per day or choose multiple ones to meditate on each day. The goal is that the more you embrace God's opinion of you, the more you will embody the life of Christ in all that you do, including your business.

1) I am a child of God (Romans 8:16)
2) I am loved by God (John 3:16)
3) I am forgiven of all my sins (Ephesians 1:7)
4) I am one in Christ (John 17:21)
5) I am the righteousness of God in Christ Jesus (2 Corinthians 5:21)
6) I am called of God (2 Timothy 1:9)
7) I am the apple of my Father's eye (Psalm 17:8)
8) I am being changed into His image (2 Corinthians 3:18)
9) I am a new creation (2 Corinthians 5:17)
10) I am the temple of the Holy Spirit (1 Corinthians 6:19)
11) I am seated with Christ in Heavenly places (Ephesians 2:6)
12) I am an heir of God and joint-heir with Jesus (Romans 8:17)
13) I am the spiritual seed of Abraham (Galatians 3:16)
14) I am redeemed from the curse of the Law (Galatians 3:13)
15) I am blessed with every spiritual blessing (Ephesians 1:3)
16) I am above and not beneath (Deuteronomy 28:13)
17) I am a lender and not a borrower (Deuteronomy 28:13)
18) I am the elect of God (Colossians 3:12)
19) I am fearfully and wonderfully made (Psalm 139:14)
20) I am free (John 8:31)
21) I am led by the Spirit of God (Romans 8:14)
22) I am more than a conqueror (Romans 8:37)
23) I am healed by His stripes (Isaiah 53:5)
24) I am walking by faith and not by sight (2 Corinthians 5:7)
25) I am a co-laborer with God (1 Corinthians 3:9)
26) I am an imitator of Jesus Christ (Ephesians 5:1)
27) I am an overcomer by the blood of the Lamb and the word of my testimony (Revelation 12:11)
28) I am delivered from the powers of darkness (Colossians 1:3)
29) I am doing all things thru Christ who strengthens me (Philippians 4:13)
30) I am living in the shalom of God (Hebrews 4:10)
31) I am victorious (2 Corinthians 2:14)

There are some many more that could be added to this list, so this is just a beginning. The additional component of this process is to write down and declare what you believe God has promised you, specific to your business present and future. Again, you want to declare these over your business everyday. You could write something similar to this:

1) I am a great husband and father.
2) I am debt free.
3) I am the possessor and facilitator of billion dollar ideas that impact billions of people.
4) I am a world renowned, highly sought after preacher of the Word of God and author.
5) I am the Marketplace Pastor and President of Kingdom Business University, which is a billion dollar business and ministry that produces marketplace apostles, prophets, evangelists, pastors and teachers who are entrepreneurs, business leaders and community change agents.
6) I am the leader of a business incubator, which has a multimillion dollar budget used to transform families and communities by incubating dreams, growing businesses and creating jobs.
7) I am a media industry influencer.

Now it's your turn…

Business Declarations

1) _____

2) _____

3) _____

4) _____

5) _____

6) _____

7) _____

8) _____

9) _____

10) _____

Now go BE who you ARE!

APPENDIX

Resources

V-STAR Quick Start Business Planning Questionnaire

V-STAR, which stands for Vision, Strategy, Target, Action Results, was created by Paul Wilson, Jr. This was developed as an outcome of more than a decade of experience as a respected advisor to corporations, small businesses, non-profits, and professionals at all levels. Some of my clients / engagements include the National Football League, Edison Electric Institute, Utility Purchasing Management Group, Georgia Minority Supplier Development Council, Indiana Utility Association, Everest College, Nevada Energy, Alabama Power, Vectren, Louisville Gas & Electric, American Electric Power, multiple small businesses, and many other organizations.

Vision:
1) What is your life purpose / calling?
2) What is your business vision?
3) What is your mission, i.e. how will you accomplish your vision?
4) How does your life purpose business vision and mission?
5) How is your vision / mission connected to advancing God's Kingdom?
6) What are the foundational values / guiding principles of your company? What are your core beliefs as it relates to your business practices?
7) What type of company culture do you want to have?

Strategy:
1) SWOT Analysis (see questions below)
2) What were your company goals last year? Did you accomplish your goals last year?
3) How easy or challenging was it to accomplish your goals?
4) What were the key factors that allowed you to accomplish your goals (internal and external)?
5) What special circumstances contributed to whether or not you accomplished your goals (internal and external)?
6) What are your goals and objectives this year? What are you five-year goals?
7) What is the time frame for this project?
8) How will you accomplish your goals?
9) What key factors have changed since last year that may have a positive or negative impact on your goals (internal and external)?
10) What resources are needed to accomplish your strategy (people, organizations, money, facilities)?
11) Who is on your team? Who are your leaders? What are their roles?

12) What is your budget?
13) How will you fund this?

Target:
1) What value are you delivering to your customers? Are you satisfying a need, want, or desire?
2) Who is your primary target market?
3) Who is your secondary target market?
4) What are the key demographics of your target market(s)?
5) What is unique/distinct about your target market(s)?
6) What unique/special circumstances impact or influence your target market(s)?
7) How will you generate sales/revenues?
8) What is your marketing strategy?
9) How will you reach your target market? Where will you do your marketing?
10) What social media platforms do you use?
11) Who are your competitors?
12) What advantages do you have over your competitors?
13) What advantages do your competitors have over you?
14) What is your pricing strategy, i.e. discount, mid-level, premium?
15) What is your slogan?

Actions:
1) What steps are you going to take to execute/initiate/implement your strategy?
2) What is your schedule?
3) When is the launch date?
4) What is your marketing schedule?
5) What is your Phase 1, 2, 3, etc?

Results:
1) What metrics have you used to measure success in the past? Were those metrics sufficient?
2) What metrics will you use to measure success this year?
3) Do new metrics need to be considered?
4) Do current metrics need to be modified or discarded?
5) How often will you measure your results?
6) What methods all you use?

SWOT Analysis Questions
Strengths in your business:
1) Areas to consider: management, branding/marketing, products/services, customer service, financial management, operations, technology, etc.
2) What's unique about your business?
3) What are your assets?
4) What do you do exceptionally well?
5) What is your business good at?
6) Personal strengths

Weaknesses in your business:
1) Areas to consider: management, branding / marketing, products / services, customer service, financial management, operations, technology, etc.
2) What are you lacking?
3) Where do you have deficiencies?
4) Where do you have performance gaps?
5) Personal weaknesses

Opportunities in the marketplace
1) Things to consider: economy, laws, technology, competition, world, event, local events, etc.
2) What is available that you can take advantage of?
3) Who can you partner with?
4) What new complementary products / services can you offer?
5) What's happening / changing in the marketplace that can help you?

Threats in the marketplace
1) Things to consider: economy, laws, technology, competition, world events, local events, etc.
2) What's happening / changing in the marketplace that can hurt you?
3) Who are your competitors?
4) What do your competitors do better than you?

V-STAR Quick Start Business Plan

Use this form as a way to summarize the work you have been doing throughout this book. This will be a snapshot that you can refer to periodically to confirm if you are on track or need to make adjustments.

Core Function	Measurement
Vision, Mission, Values *What are you aiming to accomplish?* *What are you goals?* *How will you do business?*	
Strategy *How will you accomplish your vision/mission?*	
Target Market *Who is your niche?* *How will you market to them?*	
Action Planning *What is your (re)startup plan?* *What do you need to do to get started?* *When do you need to do it?* *What resources do you need?*	
Results Management *What are my performance measurements?*	

101 Biblical Proverbs About Money

This complete list is available at www.faithandfinance.org. You can get a PDF version at their web site.

Wealth in Wisdom and Knowledge

Proverbs 2:3-4 Cry out for insight, and ask for understanding. Search for them as you would for silver; seek them like hidden treasures.

Proverbs 3:13, 14 Joyful is the person who finds wisdom, the one who gains understanding. For wisdom is more profitable than silver, and her wages are better than gold.

Proverbs 8:10, 11 Choose my instruction rather than silver, and knowledge rather than pure gold. For wisdom is far more valuable than rubies. Nothing you desire can compare with it.

Proverbs 9:10 Fear of the Lord is the foundation of wisdom. Knowledge of the Holy One results in good judgment.

Proverbs 15:16 Better to have little, with fear for the Lord, than to have great treasure and inner turmoil.

Proverbs 16:8 Better to have little, with godliness, than to be rich and dishonest.

Proverbs 16:16 How much better to get wisdom than gold, and good judgment than silver!

Proverbs 17:16 It is senseless to pay tuition to educate a fool, since he has no heart for learning.

Proverbs 20:15 Wise words are more valuable than much gold and many rubies

Hard Work

Proverbs 6:6-8 Take a lesson from the ants, you lazybones. Learn from their ways and become wise! Though they have no prince or governor or ruler to make them work, they labor hard all summer, gathering food for the winter.

Proverbs 6:10, 11 A little extra sleep, a little more slumber, a little folding of the hands to rest—then poverty will pounce on you like a bandit; scarcity will attack you like an armed robber.

Proverbs 10:4 Lazy people are soon poor; hard workers get rich.

Proverbs 10:5 A wise youth harvests in the summer, but one who sleeps during harvest is a disgrace.

Proverbs 12:11 A hard worker has plenty of food, but a person who chases fantasies has no sense.

Proverbs 13:4 Lazy people want much but get little, but those who work hard will prosper.

Proverbs 13:11 Wealth from get-rich-quick schemes quickly disappears; wealth from hard work grows over time.

Proverbs 14:23 Work brings profit, but mere talk leads to poverty!

Proverbs 20:13 If you love sleep, you will end in poverty. Keep your eyes open, and there will be plenty to eat!

Proverbs 21:5 Good planning and hard work lead to prosperity, but hasty shortcuts lead to poverty.

Proverbs 24:33, 34 A little extra sleep, a little more slumber, a little folding of the hands to rest—then poverty will pounce on you like a bandit; scarcity will attack you like an armed robber.

Proverbs 28:19 A hard worker has plenty of food, but a person who chases fantasies ends up in poverty.

Rich and Poor

Proverbs 10:15 The wealth of the rich is their fortress; the poverty of the poor is their destruction.

Proverbs 13:7 Some who are poor pretend to be rich; others who are rich pretend to be poor.

Proverbs 13:8 The rich can pay a ransom for their lives, but the poor won't even get threatened.

Proverbs 13:23 A poor person's farm may produce much food, but injustice sweeps it all away.

Proverbs 14:20 The poor are despised even by their neighbors, while the rich have many "friends."

Proverbs 17:5 Those who mock the poor insult their Maker; those who rejoice at the misfortune of others will be punished.

Proverbs 18:11 The rich think of their wealth as a strong defense; they imagine it to be a high wall of safety.

Proverbs 18:23 The poor plead for mercy; the rich answer with insults.

Proverbs 19:7 The relatives of the poor despise them; how much more will their friends avoid them! Though the poor plead with them, their friends are gone.

Proverbs 21:17 Those who love pleasure become poor; those who love wine and luxury will never be rich.

Proverbs 22:2 The rich and poor have this in common: The Lord made them both.

Proverbs 28:3 A poor person who oppresses the poor is like a pounding rain that destroys the crops.

Proverbs 28:6 Better to be poor and honest than to be dishonest and rich.

Proverbs 28:11 Rich people may think they are wise, but a poor person with discernment can see right through them.

Greed

Proverbs 1:19 Such is the fate of all who are greedy for money; it robs them of life.

Proverbs 15:27 Greed brings grief to the whole family, but those who hate bribes will live.

Proverbs 22:16 A person who gets ahead by oppressing the poor or by showering gifts on the rich will end in poverty.

Proverbs 22:22-23 Don't rob the poor just because you can, or exploit the needy in court. For the Lord is their defender. He will ruin anyone who ruins them.

Proverbs 23:4 Don't wear yourself out trying to get rich. Be wise enough to know when to quit.

Proverbs 28:8 Income from charging high interest rates will end up in the pocket of someone who is kind to the poor.

Proverbs 28:20 The trustworthy person will get a rich reward, but a person who wants quick riches will get into trouble.

Proverbs 28:22 Greedy people try to get rich quick but don't realize they're headed for poverty.

Proverbs 28:25 Greed causes fighting; trusting the Lord leads to prosperity.

Provision

Proverbs 3:5, 6 Trust in the Lord with all your heart; do not depend on your own understanding. Seek his will in all you do, and he will show you which path to take.

Proverbs 11:26 People curse those who hoard their grain, but they bless the one who sells in time of need.

Proverbs 11:28 Trust in your money and down you go! But the godly flourish like leaves in spring.

Proverbs 19:14 Fathers can give their sons an inheritance of houses and wealth, but only the Lord can give an understanding wife.

Proverbs 30:7-9 O God, I beg two favors from you; let me have them before I die. First, help me never to tell a lie. Second, give me neither poverty nor riches! Give me just enough to satisfy my needs. For if I grow rich, I may deny you and say, "Who is the Lord?" And if I am too poor, I may steal and thus insult God's holy name.

Giving

Proverbs 3:27 Do not withhold good from those who deserve it when it's in your power to help them.

Proverbs 11:24 Give freely and become more wealthy; be stingy and lose everything.

Proverbs 11:25 The generous will prosper; those who refresh others will themselves be refreshed.

Proverbs 14:21 It is a sin to belittle one's neighbor; blessed are those who help the poor.

Proverbs 14:31 Those who oppress the poor insult their Maker, but helping the poor honors him.

Proverbs 19:17 If you help the poor, you are lending to the Lord— and he will repay you!

Proverbs 22:9 Blessed are those who are generous, because they feed the poor.

Proverbs 28:27 Whoever gives to the poor will lack nothing, but those who close their eyes to poverty will be cursed.

Wealth

Proverbs 3:9, 10 Honor the Lord with your wealth and with the best part of everything you produce. Then he will fill your barns with grain, and your vats will overflow with good wine.

Proverbs 8:18-21 I [wisdom] have riches and honor, as well as enduring wealth and justice. My gifts are better than gold, even the purest gold, my wages better than sterling silver! I walk in righteousness, in paths of justice. Those who love me inherit wealth. I will fill their treasuries.

Proverbs 10:22 The blessing of the Lord makes a person rich, and he adds no sorrow with it.

Proverbs 14:24 Wealth is a crown for the wise; the effort of fools yields only foolishness.

Proverbs 19:4 Wealth makes many "friends"; poverty drives them all away.

Proverbs 21:6 Wealth created by a lying tongue is a vanishing mist and a deadly trap.

Proverbs 22:4 True humility and fear of the Lord lead to riches, honor, and long life.

Proverbs 23:5 In the blink of an eye wealth disappears, for it will sprout wings and fly away like an eagle.

Debt and Lending

Proverbs 11:15 There's danger in putting up security for a stranger's debt; it's safer not to guarantee another person's debt.

Proverbs 17:18 It's poor judgment to guarantee another person's debt or put up security for a friend.

Proverbs 22:7 Just as the rich rule the poor, so the borrower is servant to the lender.

Proverbs 22:26, 27 Don't agree to guarantee another person's debt or put up security for someone else. If you can't pay it, even your bed will be snatched from under you.

Proverbs 27:13 Get security from someone who guarantees a stranger's debt. Get a deposit if he does it for foreigners.

Stewardship and Investments

Proverbs 10:16 The earnings of the godly enhance their lives, but evil people squander their money on sin.

Proverbs 13:22 Good people leave an inheritance to their grandchildren, but the sinner's wealth passes to the godly.

Proverbs 20:21 An inheritance obtained too early in life is not a blessing in the end.

Proverbs 27:23, 24 Know the state of your flocks, and put your heart into caring for your herds, for riches don't last forever, and the crown might not be passed to the next generation.

Proverbs 31:16 She goes to inspect a field and buys it; with her earnings she plants a vineyard.

Proverbs 31:20 She extends a helping hand to the poor and opens her arms to the needy.

Righteous Living

Proverbs 10:2 Tainted wealth has no lasting value, but right living can save your life.

Proverbs 11:4 Riches won't help on the day of judgment, but right living can save you from death.

Proverbs 11:18 Evil people get rich for the moment, but the reward of the godly will last.

Proverbs 13:21 Trouble chases sinners, while blessings reward the righteous.

Proverbs 15:6 There is treasure in the house of the godly, but the earnings of the wicked bring trouble.

Proverbs 17:3 Fire tests the purity of silver and gold, but the Lord tests the heart.

Proverbs 19:1 Better to be poor and honest than to be dishonest and a fool.

Proverbs 22:1 Choose a good reputation over great riches; being held in high esteem is better than silver or gold.

72 Scriptures on Prosperity

This list was compiled by Michael G. Holmes. Learn more at www.michaelgholmes.com.

Wealth by Design

Genesis 12: 1-3 (AMP) "NOW [in Haran] the Lord said to Abram, 'Go for yourself [for your own advantage] away from your country, from your relatives and your father's house, to the land that I will show you. And I will make of you a great nation, and I will bless you [with abundant increase of favors] and make your name famous and distinguished, and you will be a blessing [dispensing good to others]. And I will bless those who bless you [who confer prosperity or happiness upon you] and curse him who curses or uses insolent language toward you; in you will all the families and kindred of the earth be blessed [and by you they will bless themselves].'"

1 Samuel 2:7-9 (NKJV) "The Lord makes poor and makes rich; He brings low and lifts up. He raises the poor from the dust And lifts the beggar from the ash heap, To set them among princes And make them inherit the throne of glory. For the pillars of the earth are the Lord's, And He has set the world upon them. He will guard the feet of His saints, But the wicked shall be silent in darkness. For by strength no man shall prevail."

1 Chronicles 29:11-13 (NKJV) "Yours, O Lord, is the greatness, The power and the glory, The victory and the majesty; For all that is in heaven and in earth is Yours; Yours is the kingdom, O Lord, And You are exalted as head over all. Both riches and honor come from You, And You reign over all. In Your hand is power and might; In Your hand it is to make great And to give strength to all. Now therefore, our God, We thank You And praise Your glorious name."

Psalms 35:27 (KJV) "Let them shout for joy, and be glad, that favour my righteous cause: yea, let them say continually, 'Let the LORD be magnified, which hath pleasure in the prosperity of his servant.'"

Proverbs 10:22 (KJV) "The blessing of the LORD, it maketh rich, and he addeth no sorrow with it."

Proverbs 13:22 (AMP) "A good man leaves an inheritance [of moral stability and goodness] to his children's children, and the wealth of the sinner [finds its way eventually] into the hands of the righteous, for whom it was laid up."

Ecclesiastes 2:26 (NIV) "To the person who pleases him, God gives wisdom, knowledge and happiness, but to the sinner he gives the task of gathering and storing up wealth to hand it over to the one who pleases God. This too is meaningless, a chasing after the wind."

Ecclesiastes 5:19 (NKJV) "As for every man to whom God has given riches and wealth, and given him power to eat of it, to receive his heritage and rejoice in his labor—this is the gift of God."

Romans 8:32 (KJV) "He that spared not His own Son, but delivered Him up for us all, how shall He not with Him also freely give us all things?"
3 John 1:2 (KJV) "Beloved, I wish above all things that thou mayest prosper and be in health, even as thy soul prospereth."

Wealth by Giving
Deuteronomy 15:7-10 (MSG) "When you happen on someone who's in trouble or needs help among your people with whom you live in this land that God, your God, is giving you, don't look the other way pretending you don't see him. Don't keep a tight grip on your purse. No. Look at him, open your purse, lend whatever and as much as he needs. Don't count the cost. Don't listen to that selfish voice saying, 'It's almost the seventh year, the year of All-Debts-Are-Canceled,' and turn aside and leave your needy neighbor in the lurch, refusing to help him. He'll call God's attention to you and your blatant sin. Give freely and spontaneously. Don't have a stingy heart. The way you handle matters like this triggers God, your God's, blessing in everything you do, all your work and ventures."
1 Kings 8-15 (NLT) "Then the LORD said to Elijah, 'Go and live in the village of Zarephath, near the city of Sidon. There is a widow there who will feed you. I have given her My instructions.' So he went to Zarephath. As he arrived at the gates of the village, he saw a widow gathering sticks, and he asked her, 'Would you please bring me a cup of water?' As she was going to get it, he called to her, 'Bring me a bite of bread, too.'
But she said, 'I swear by the LORD your God that I don't have a single piece of bread in the house. And I have only a handful of flour left in the jar and a little cooking oil in the bottom of the jug. I was just gathering a few sticks to cook this last meal, and then my son and I will die.' But Elijah said to her, 'Don't be afraid! Go ahead and cook that 'last meal,' but bake me a little loaf of bread first. Afterward there will still be enough food for you and your son. For this is what the LORD, the God of Israel, says: 'There will always be plenty of flour and oil left in your containers until the time when the LORD sends rain and the crops grow again!' So she did as Elijah said, and she and Elijah and her son continued to eat from her supply of flour and oil for many days."
Job 42:10 (NKJV) "And the Lord restored Job's losses when he prayed for his friends. Indeed the Lord gave Job twice as much as he had before."
Proverbs 3:9-10 (NKJV) "Honor the Lord with your possessions, and with the firstfruits of all your increase; so your barns will be filled with plenty, and your vats will overflow with new wine."
Proverbs 11:24-25 (NLT) "Give freely and become more wealthy; be stingy and lose everything. The generous will prosper; those who refresh others will themselves be refreshed."
Proverbs 28:27 (NLT) "Whoever gives to the poor will lack nothing. But a

curse will come upon those who close their eyes to poverty."

Malachi 3:8-12 (AMP) "Will a man rob or defraud God? Yet you rob and defraud Me. But you say, In what way do we rob or defraud You? [You have withheld your] tithes and offerings. You are cursed with the curse, for you are robbing Me, even this whole nation. Bring all the tithes (the whole tenth of your income) into the storehouse, that there may be food in My house, and prove Me now by it, says the Lord of hosts, if I will not open the windows of heaven for you and pour you out a blessing, that there shall not be room enough to receive it. And I will rebuke the devourer [insects and plagues] for your sakes and he shall not destroy the fruits of your ground, neither shall your vine drop its fruit before the time in the field, says the Lord of hosts. And all nations shall call you happy and blessed, for you shall be a land of delight, says the Lord of hosts."

Luke 6:38 (KJV) "Give, and it shall be given unto you; good measure, pressed down, and shaken together, and running over, shall men give into your bosom. For with the same measure that ye mete withal it shall be measured to you again."

2 Corinthians 9:6-15 (AMP) "[Remember] this: he who sows sparingly and grudgingly will also reap sparingly and grudgingly, and he who sows generously [that blessings may come to someone] will also reap generously and with blessings. Let each one [give] as he has made up his own mind and purposed in his heart, not reluctantly or sorrowfully or under compulsion, for God loves (He takes pleasure in, prizes above other things, and is unwilling to abandon or to do without) a cheerful (joyous, "prompt to do it") giver [whose heart is in his giving]. And God is able to make all grace (every favor and earthly blessing) come to you in abundance, so that you may always and under all circumstances and whatever the need be self-sufficient [possessing enough to require no aid or support and furnished in abundance for every good work and charitable donation].

As it is written, He [the benevolent person] scatters abroad; He gives to the poor; His deeds of justice and goodness and kindness and benevolence will go on and endure forever! And [God] Who provides seed for the sower and bread for eating will also provide and multiply your [resources for] sowing and increase the fruits of your righteousness [which manifests itself in active goodness, kindness, and charity]. Thus you will be enriched in all things and in every way, so that you can be generous, and [your generosity as it is] administered by us will bring forth thanksgiving to God.

For the service that the ministering of this fund renders does not only fully supply what is lacking to the saints (God's people), but it also overflows in many [cries of] thanksgiving to God. Because at [your] standing of the test of this ministry, they will glorify God for your loyalty and obedience to the Gospel of Christ which you confess, as well as for your generous-hearted liberality to them and to all [the other needy ones]. And they yearn for you while they pray for you, because of the surpassing measure of God's grace (His favor and mercy and spiritual blessing which is shown forth) in you. Now thanks be to God for His Gift, [precious] beyond telling [His indescribable, inexpressible, free Gift]!"

Phillipians 4:15-19 (AMP) "And you Philippians yourselves well know that in the early days of the Gospel ministry, when I left Macedonia, no church (assembly) entered into partnership with me and opened up [a debit and credit] account in giving and receiving except you only. For even in Thessalonica you sent [me contributions] for my needs, not only once but a second time. Not that I seek or am eager for [your] gift, but I do seek and am eager for the fruit which increases to your credit [the harvest of blessing that is accumulating to your account]. But I have [your full payment] and more; I have everything I need and am amply supplied, now that I have received from Epaphroditus the gifts you sent me. [They are the] fragrant odor of an offering and sacrifice which God welcomes and in which He delights. And my God will liberally supply (fill to the full) your every need according to His riches in glory in Christ Jesus."

Wealth by Trust

Deuteronomy 8:18 (NKJV) "And you shall remember the Lord your God, for it is He who gives you power to get wealth, that He may establish His covenant which He swore to your fathers, as it is this day."

Deuteronomy 30:9 (NKJV) "The Lord your God will make you abound in all the work of your hand, in the fruit of your body, in the increase of your livestock, and in the produce of your land for good. For the Lord will again rejoice over you for good as He rejoiced over your fathers."

Joshua 1:8-9 (NKJV) "This Book of the Law shall not depart from your mouth, but you shall meditate in it day and night, that you may observe to do according to all that is written in it. For then you will make your way prosperous, and then you will have good success. Have I not commanded you? Be strong and of good courage; do not be afraid, nor be dismayed, for the Lord your God is with you wherever you go."

Psalms 1:1-3 (The Living Bible) "Oh, the joys of those who do not follow evil men's advice, who do not hang around with sinners, scoffing at the things of God: But they delight in doing everything God wants them to, and day and night are always meditating on His Laws and thinking about ways to follow Him more closely. They are like trees along a river bank bearing luscious fruit each season without fail. Their leaves never wither, and all they do shall prosper."

Psalms 84:11 (NKJV) "For the Lord God is a sun and shield; The Lord will give grace and glory; No good thing will He withhold From those who walk uprightly."

Proverbs 22:4 (KJV) "By humility and the fear of the Lord are riches, and honour, and life."

Psalms 112:1-9 (AMP) "PRAISE THE Lord! (Hallelujah!) Blessed (happy, fortunate, to be envied) is the man who fears (reveres and worships) the Lord, who delights greatly in His commandments. His [spiritual] offspring shall be mighty upon earth; the generation of the upright shall be blessed. Prosperity and welfare are in his house, and his righteousness endures forever.

Light arises in the darkness for the upright, gracious, compassionate, and just [who are in right standing with God]. It is well with the man who deals generously and lends, who conducts his affairs with justice. He will not be moved forever; the [uncompromisingly] righteous (the upright, in right standing with God) shall be in everlasting remembrance. He shall not be afraid of evil tidings; his heart is firmly fixed, trusting (leaning on and being confident) in the Lord.

His heart is established and steady, he will not be afraid while he waits to see his desire established upon his adversaries. He has distributed freely [he has given to the poor and needy]; his righteousness (uprightness and right standing with God) endures forever; his horn shall be exalted in honor."

Psalms 118:25 (KJV) "Save now, I beseech thee, O LORD: O LORD, I beseech thee, send now prosperity."

Psalms 144:15 (AMP) "Happy and blessed are the people who are in such a case; yes, happy (blessed, fortunate, prosperous, to be envied) are the people whose God is the Lord!"

Proverbs 28:25 (NLT) "Greed causes fighting; trusting the LORD leads to prosperity."

Isaiah 1:19 (The Living Bible) "If you will only let Me help you, if you will only obey, then I will make you rich!"

Isaiah 48:18 (AMP) "Thus says the Lord, your Redeemer, the Holy One of Israel: 'I am the Lord your God, Who teaches you to profit, Who leads you in the way that you should go.'"

Jeremiah 17:5-8 (AMP) "Thus says the Lord: 'Cursed [with great evil] is the strong man who trusts in and relies on frail man, making weak [human] flesh his arm, and whose mind and heart turn aside from the Lord. For he shall be like a shrub or a person naked and destitute in the desert; and he shall not see any good come, but shall dwell in the parched places in the wilderness, in an uninhabited salt land. [Most] blessed is the man who believes in, trusts in, and relies on the Lord, and whose hope and confidence the Lord is. For he shall be like a tree planted by the waters that spreads out its roots by the river; and it shall not see and fear when heat comes; but its leaf shall be green. It shall not be anxious and full of care in the year of drought, nor shall it cease yielding fruit.'"

2 Chronicles 31:20-21 (The Living Bible) "In this way King Hezekiah handled the distribution throughout all of Judah, doing what was just and fair in the sight of the Lord his God. He worked very hard to encourage respect for the Temple, the law, and godly living, and was very successful."

Wealth By Trial

Psalm 66:10-12 (KJV) "For thou, O God, hast proved us: thou hast tried us, as silver is tried. Thou broughtest us into the net; thou laidst affliction upon our loins. Thou hast caused men to ride over our heads; we went through fire and through water: but thou broughtest us out into a wealthy place."

Psalm 71:20-21 (KJV) "Thou, which hast shewed me great and sore troubles, shalt quicken me again, and shalt bring me up again from the depths of the earth. Thou shalt increase my greatness, and comfort me on every side."

Wealth With Wisdom

Proverbs 3:13-16 (KJV) "Happy is the man that findeth wisdom, and the man that getteth understanding. For the merchandise of it is better than the merchandise of silver, and the gain thereof than fine gold. She is more precious than rubies: and all the things thou canst desire are not to be compared unto her. Length of days is in her right hand; and in her left hand riches and honour."

Proverbs 8: 17-19 (KJV) "I (wisdom) love them that love me; and those that seek me early shall find me. Riches and honour are with me; yea, durable riches and righteousness. My fruit is better than gold, yea, than fine gold; and my revenue than choice silver."

Proverbs 21:5 (NLT) "Good planning and hard work lead to prosperity, but hasty shortcuts lead to poverty."

Proverbs 21:17 (The Living Bible) "A man who loves pleasure becomes poor; wine and luxury are not the way to riches."

Proverbs 24:3-4 (KJV) "Through wisdom is an house builded; and by understanding it is established: And by knowledge shall the chambers be filled with all precious and pleasant riches."

Proverbs 24:27 (The Living Bible) "Develop your business first before building your house."

Ecclesiastes 7:11-14 (NLT) "Wisdom is even better when you have money. Both are a benefit as you go through life. Wisdom and money can get you almost anything, but only wisdom can save your life. Accept the way God does things, for who can straighten what he has made crooked? Enjoy prosperity while you can, but when hard times strike, realize that both come from God. Remember that nothing is certain in this life."

Jeremiah 29:11 (NIV) "For I know the plans I have for you,' declares the LORD, 'plans to prosper you and not to harm you, plans to give you hope and a future.'"

Wealth by Good Stewardship

Proverbs 21:5 (NASB) "The thoughts of the diligent tend only to plenty; but the thoughts of everyone who is hasty only to poverty."

Proverbs 22:3 (NASB) "A prudent one foresees the evil and hides himself, but the simple pass on and are punished."

Proverbs 27: 23-27 (ESV) "Know well the condition of your flocks, and give attention to your herds, for riches do not last forever; and does a crown endure to all generations? When the grass is gone and the new growth appears and the vegetation of the mountains is gathered, the lambs will provide your clothing, and the goats the price of a field. There will be enough goats' milk for your food, for the food of your household and maintenance for your girls."

Proverbs 28:20 (NASB) "A faithful man will abound with blessings, but he who makes haste to be rich will not go unpunished."

Wealth by Planning

Genesis 41:28-36 (CEV) "It is just as I said—God has shown what he intends to do. For seven years Egypt will have more than enough grain, but that will be followed by seven years when there won't be enough. The good years of plenty will be forgotten, and everywhere in Egypt people will be starving. The famine will be so bad that no one will remember that once there had been plenty. God has given you two dreams to let you know that he has definitely decided to do this and that he will do it soon. "Your Majesty, you should find someone who is wise and will know what to do, so that you can put him in charge of all Egypt. Then appoint some other officials to collect one fifth of every crop harvested in Egypt during the seven years when there is plenty. Give them the power to collect the grain during those good years and to store it in your cities. It can be stored until it is needed during the seven years when there won't be enough grain in Egypt. This will keep the country from being destroyed because of the lack of food."

Proverbs 13:16 (The Living Bible) "A wise man thinks ahead; a fool doesn't, and even brags about it!"

Proverbs 22:3 (NASB) "The prudent sees the evil and hides himself, but the naive go on, and are punished for it."

Proverbs 21:5 (NASB) "The plans of the diligent lead surely to advantage, but everyone who is hasty comes surely to poverty."

Wealth For Good (or God's) Purpose

1 Chronicles 29:1-9 (NLT) "When King David turned to the entire assembly and said, 'My son Solomon, whom God has clearly chosen as the next king of Israel, is still young and inexperienced. The work ahead of him is enormous, for the Temple he will build is not for mere mortals—it is for the Lord God himself! Using every resource at my command, I have gathered as much as I could for building the Temple of my God. Now there is enough gold, silver, bronze, iron, and wood, as well as great quantities of onyx, other precious stones, costly jewels, and all kinds of fine stone and marble. And now, because of my devotion to the Temple of my God, I am giving all of my own private treasures of gold and silver to help in the construction.

This is in addition to the building materials I have already collected for his holy Temple. I am donating more than 112 tons of gold from Ophir and 262 tons of refined silver to be used for overlaying the walls of the buildings and for the other gold and silver work to be done by the craftsmen. Now then, who will follow my example and give offerings to the Lord today?'

Then the family leaders, the leaders of the tribes of Israel, the generals and captains of the army, and the king's administrative officers all gave willingly. For the construction of the Temple of God, they gave about 188 tons of gold, 10,000 gold coins, 375 tons of silver, 675 tons of bronze, and 3,750 tons of iron. They also contributed numerous precious stones, which were deposited in the treasury of the house of the Lord under the care of Jehiel, a descendant of Gershon. The people rejoiced over the offerings, for they had given freely and wholeheartedly to the Lord, and King David was filled with joy."

Proverbs 10:16 (The Living Bible) "The good man's earnings advance the cause of righteousness. The evil man squanders his on sin."

Acts 2:42-46 (NLT) "All the believers devoted themselves to the apostles' teaching, and to fellowship, and to sharing in meals (including the Lord's Supper), and to prayer. A deep sense of awe came over them all, and the apostles performed many miraculous signs and wonders. And all the believers met together in one place and shared everything they had. They sold their property and possessions and shared the money with those in need. They worshiped together at the Temple each day, met in homes for the Lord's Supper, and shared their meals with great joy and generosity."

Warnings About Wealth

Proverbs 11:4 (NKJV) "Riches do not profit in the day of wrath, but righteousness delivers from death."

Proverbs 11:28 (The Living Bible) "Trust in your money and down you go! Trust in God and flourish as a tree!"

Proverbs 13:7 (The Living Bible) "Some rich people are poor, and some poor people have great wealth!"

Proverbs 13:8 (AMP) "A rich man can buy his way out of threatened death by paying a ransom, but the poor man does not even have to listen to threats [from the envious]."

Proverbs 15:16 (The Living Bible) "Better a little with reverence for God, than great treasure and trouble with it."

Proverbs 23:4-5 (NIV) "Do not wear yourself out to get rich; have the wisdom to show restraint. Cast but a glance at riches, and they are gone, for they will surely sprout wings and fly off to the sky like an eagle."

Proverbs 22:1-2 (TNIV) "A good name is more desirable than great riches; to be esteemed is better than silver or gold. Rich and poor have this in common: The Lord is the Maker of them all."

Jeremiah 9:23-24 (NKJV) "Thus says the Lord: 'Let not the wise man glory in his wisdom, Let not the mighty man glory in his might, Nor let the rich man glory in his riches; But let him who glories glory in this, That he understands and knows Me, That I am the Lord, exercising lovingkindness, judgment, and righteousness in the earth. For in these I delight,' says the Lord."

Matthew 6:19-24 (NKJV) "Do not lay up for yourselves treasures on earth, where moth and rust destroy and where thieves break in and steal; but lay up for yourselves treasures in heaven, where neither moth nor rust destroys and where thieves do not break in and steal. For where your treasure is, there your heart will be also. "The lamp of the body is the eye. If therefore your eye is good, your whole body will be full of light. But if your eye is bad, your whole body will be full of darkness. If therefore the light that is in you is darkness, how great is that darkness! "No one can serve two masters; for either he will hate the one and love the other, or else he will be loyal to the one and despise the other. You cannot serve God and mammon (money)."

Matthew 16:26 (NIV) "What good will it be for a man if he gains the whole world, yet forfeits his soul? Or what can a man give in exchange for his soul?"

Luke 12:13 (NKJV) "And He said to them, 'Take heed and beware of covetousness, for one's life does not consist in the abundance of the things he possesses.'"

Acts 5:1-11 (MSG) "But a man named Ananias—his wife, Sapphira, conniving in this with him—sold a piece of land, secretly kept part of the price for himself, and then brought the rest to the apostles and made an offering of it. Peter said, 'Ananias, how did Satan get you to lie to the Holy Spirit and secretly keep back part of the price of the field? Before you sold it, it was all yours, and after you sold it, the money was yours to do with as you wished. So what got into you to pull a trick like this? You didn't lie to men but to God.' Ananias, when he heard those words, fell down dead. That put the fear of God into everyone who heard of it. The younger men went right to work and wrapped him up, then carried him out and buried him. Not more than three hours later, his wife, knowing nothing of what had happened, came in.

Peter said, 'Tell me, were you given this price for your field?'

'Yes,' she said, 'that price.' Peter responded, 'What's going on here that you connived to conspire against the Spirit of the Master? The men who buried your husband are at the door, and you're next.' No sooner were the words out of his mouth than she also fell down, dead. When the young men returned they found her body. They carried her out and buried her beside her husband.

By this time the whole church and, in fact, everyone who heard of these things had a healthy respect for God. They knew God was not to be trifled with."

1 Timothy 6:6-11 (NLT) "Now godliness with contentment is great gain. For we brought nothing into this world, and it is certain we can carry nothing out. And having food and clothing, with these we shall be content. But those who desire to be rich fall into temptation and a snare, and into many foolish and harmful lusts which drown men in destruction and perdition. For the love of money is a root of all kinds of evil, for which some have strayed from the faith in their greediness, and pierced themselves through with many sorrows. But you, O man of God, flee these things and pursue righteousness, godliness, faith, love, patience, gentleness."

1 Timothy 6:17-19 (NIV) "Command those who are rich in this present world not to be arrogant nor to put their hope in wealth, which is so uncertain, but to put their hope in God, who richly provides us with everything for our enjoyment. Command them to do good, to be rich in good deeds, and to be generous and willing to share. In this way they will lay up treasure for themselves as a firm foundation for the coming age, so that they may take hold of the life that is truly life."

1 John 3:17 (NIV) "If anyone has material possessions and sees his brother in need but has no pity on him, how can the love of God be in him?"

Revelation 3:17-18 (GNT) "You say, 'I am rich and well off; I have all I need.' But you do not know how miserable and pitiful you are! You are poor, naked, and blind. I advise you, then, to buy gold from Me, pure gold, in order to be rich. Buy also white clothing to dress yourself and cover up your shameful nakedness. Buy also some ointment to put on your eyes, so that you may see."

Online Resources
A Real Change (social media strategies), www.arealchange.com
Business as Mission Network, www.businessasmissionnetwork.com
Eden's Bridge, www.edensbridge.org
Entrepreneur.com, www.entrepreneur.com
Faith and Finance, www.faithandfinance.org
Fast Company, www.fastcompany.com
Fortune Small Business, http://money.cnn.com/smbusiness
The High Calling, www.thehighcalling.org
Inc. Magazine, www.inc.com
Institute for Entrepreneurial Thinking, www.entrethinking.com
Institute for Faith, Work, and Economics, www.tifwe.org
Institute for Social Entrepreneurs, www.socialent.org
Kauffman Foundation, www.eventuring.org
Kingdom Business University, www.kingdombusinessuniversity.com
Kingdom Driven Entrepreneur, www.kingdomdrivenentrepreneur.com
Kings and Priests, www.kings-priests.org
Marketplace Leaders, www.marketplaceleaders.org
Net Impact, www.netimpact.org
Small Business Administration, www.sba.gov
Small Business CEO, www.smbceo.com
Small Business Trends, www.smallbiztrends.com
Stanford Social Innovation Review, www.ssireview.org
Women's Business Enterprise National Council, www.wbenc.org

Resource Books
40-Day Coaching Guide: A Spiritual Journal for Entrepreneurs, Patrice Tsague
Anointed for Business, Ed Silvoso
Business by the Book, Larry Burkett
The Complete Idiot's Guide to Low-Cost Startups, Gail Reid
Cracking the Millionaire Code, Mark Victor Hansen & Robert Allen
The E-Myth Revisited, Michael Gerber
Eden's Bridge: The Marketplace in Creation and Mission, David B. Doty
Entrepreneurial Faith, Kirbyjon Caldwell & Walt Kallestad
The End of Poverty, Jeffrey Sachs
Faith Based Marketing: The Guide to Reaching 140 Million Christian Customers, Bob Hutchins & Greg Stielstra
God is at Work, Ken Eldred
Good to Great, Jim Collins
Great Commission Companies, Steve Rundle & Tom Steffen
Jesus, Entrepreneur: Using Ancient Wisdom to Live and Launch Your Dreams, Laurie Beth Jones
Kingdom Agenda, Dr. Tony Evans

Kingdom Calling: Vocational Stewardship for the Common Good, Amy L. Sherman
The Kingdom Driven Entrepreneur: Doing Business God's Way, Shae Bynes &
  Antonina Geer
*The Kingdom Driven Entrepreneur's Guide To Fearless Business Finance by Antonina
  Geer & Shae Bynes*
*The Kingdom Driven Entrepreneur's Guide to Pricing With Purpose by Shae Bynes and
  Antonina Geer*
Leadership Bible, John Maxwell
Marketing Like Jesus, Darren Paul Shearer
Marketplace Christianity, Robert Fraser
My Business, My Mission, Doug Seebeck
*Take Control of Your Financial Destiny: 9 Christian Entrepreneurship Principles to
  Developing a God-Inspired Business,* Dr. Amos Johnson, Jr.
The MBE Revolution: Mission Based Entrepreneur, Eric Bahme
Nothing But a Jar of Oil, Patrice Tsague & Melvin Mooring
On Kingdom Business, Tetsunao Yamamori & Kenneth A. Eldred
Small Giants, Bo Burlingham

ABOUT THE AUTHOR

As a chosen igniter for those who yearn for a more purposeful, passionate, and prosperous life, Paul Wilson Jr. is deemed the "Dream Catalyst" for such transformation. He has focused his life on inspiring people to profitably integrate the values and benefits of entrepreneurial thinking into every area of their lives. He has been a champion for spiritual empowerment, economic advancement, and community development for more than a decade.

Paul is the President of Kingdom Business University, which trains Christian CEOs to grow profitable and sustainable businesses by teaching innovative best practices built on eternal Biblical principles. Individually, he provides organizational development consulting and leadership coaching to highly motivated, high potential Christian CEOs and startups who desire to grow businesses that accomplish significant financial, spiritual, and community impact in the world.

His first book, *Dream B.I.G. in 3D: How to Pursue a Bold, Innovative God-Inspired Life!*, has helped countless numbers of people transfer the concept of a fulfilling life purpose into a meaningful reality. As a result of his strong, diverse background in small business development, leadership development, supply chain management, organizational development, and management consulting, he has consulted or spoken to several organizations including the National Football League (NFL), Fortune 500 Companies, trade organizations, small businesses, and several churches and schools all over the country.

He lives in Atlanta with his amazing wife, Shawnice, and their four exceptional children.

To learn more about how Paul can help your business maximize your Kingdom calling, please visit www.paulwilsonjr.com.

www.ingramcontent.com/pod-product-compliance
Lightning Source LLC
Chambersburg PA
CBHW070524200326
41519CB00013B/2928